Fast Track UML 2.0

KENDALL SCOTT

Fast Track UML 2.0
Copyright © 2004 by Kendall Scott

ISBN (pbk): 1-59059-320-0

Printed and bound in the United States of America 12345678910

Technical Reviewer: Doug Holland

Editorial Board: Steve Anglin, Dan Appleman, Gary Cornell, James Cox, Tony Davis, John Franklin, Chris Mills, Steve Rycroft, Dominic Shakeshaft, Julian Skinner, Jim Sumser, Karen Watterson, Gavin Wray, John Zukowski

Assistant Publisher: Grace Wong

Project Manager: Kylie Johnston

Copy Editor: John Edwards

Production Manager: Kari Brooks

Proofreader: Katie Stence

Compositor: ContentWorks

Cover Designer: Kurt Krames

Manufacturing Manager: Tom Debolski

Distributed to the book trade in the United States by Springer-Verlag New York, Inc., 175 Fifth Avenue, New York, NY, 10010 and outside the United States by Springer-Verlag GmbH & Co. KG, Tiergartenstr. 17, 69112 Heidelberg, Germany.

In the United States: phone 1-800-SPRINGER, email orders@springer-ny.com, or visit http://www.springer-ny.com. Outside the United States: fax +49 6221 345229, email orders@springer.de, or visit http://www.springer.de.

For information on translations, please contact Apress directly at 2560 Ninth Street, Suite 219, Berkeley, CA 94710. Phone 510-549-5930, fax 510-549-5939, email info@apress.com, or visit http://www.apress.com.

Contents at a Glance

Contents

Acknowledgments

I'D LIKE TO ACKNOWLEDGE THE FOLLOWING PEOPLE for having the patience to put up with the various eccentricities of this semistarving author: John Edwards, for doing such a fine job of copyediting; Doug Holland, for providing a fair and balanced technical review; Kylie Johnston, who continued to manage the project despite some contentious commentary from yours truly; and John Zukowski, for signing me to the deal in the first place and also for assorted helpful semi-technical commentary. I'd also like to thank the various and sundry Apress staff who contributed to the effort to get this to press. Finally, I must acknowledge my current muse, Jennifer Garner; it may appear at first glance that Ms. Garner doesn't offer any particularly muse-like qualities, but anyone who has seen Sydney Bristow in action knows what I'm talking about, I trust.

Kendall Scott
Harrison, Tennessee
March 2004
kendall@kendallscott.com
http://kendallscott.com

Introduction

Why This Book?

The Superstructure portion of the UML 2.0 specification with which I've been working is 7811 pages long. (Actually, it's "only" 632 pages long, but the point is that it's big.) This is the document that contains most of the "meat" that comprises the UML. However, the document is rather impenetrable for anyone who's not a "modeling junkie," which is basically why I wrote this book. In other words, I slogged my way through the spec so you don't have to.

The result is a book that's aimed at a somewhat more sophisticated audience than my previous UML book.[1] I'm assuming a certain level of knowledge of visual modeling in general; it's probably helpful if you know something about UML 1.*x*, too, but that's certainly not a requirement. I haven't done any "here's what's new in this version of UML" comparisons—I've just jumped in and taken a fresh look.

Since the UML is, after all, a visual language, there are lots of diagrams. I've offered light supplementary text for most of them; my hope is that the examples I've chosen explain themselves for the most part. Where I have particular expertise over and above what the UML is specific about—discovering classes and writing use case text—I offer what I hope is useful advice. Where I don't have particular expertise—anything related to components, for instance—I provide references to books that I've found helpful over the past several years. (I was actually coauthoring a book on component-based development for a while, but that book has not yet been published. It may come back to life; watch for it in your bookstore!)

I made my living as a technical writer for 16 years, translating complicated subject matter into reader-friendly documents and manuals. Now I earn my keep writing books and working as a trainer and mentor, teaching people about the UML and about the approach to software development that Rosenberg and Scott[2] advocate. I'd like to think that this book reflects my experience and—hey, why not?—wisdom.

---

[1] Kendall Scott, *UML Explained* (Boston, MA: Addison-Wesley, 2001).

[2] Doug Rosenberg with Kendall Scott, *Use Case Driven Object Modeling with UML* (Boston, MA: Addison-Wesley, 1999).

Organization of This Book

Chapter 1, Classes, explores how to do basic modeling of things and concepts in the real world. The chapter includes extensive detail on how to record details of classes as well as more complex structures involving classes. This chapter also includes advice on how to discover classes.

Chapter 2, Class Relationships, explores the various kinds of relationships among classes, which provide the foundation for the structure of a new system. The focus is on the three major relationship types: associations, aggregations, and dependencies.

Chapter 3, Class and Object Diagrams, provides various examples of the diagrams that show classes and their relationships. The chapter also discusses object diagrams, which capture aspects of an executing system as "snapshots."

Chapter 4, Use Cases, describes the primary means by which you can use the UML to capture functional requirements. These requirements are expressed in terms of the specific actions that external entities and the system perform in executing required and optional behavior. The chapter also offers advice on how to write robust use case text.

Chapter 5, Packages, describes the means by which you can use the UML to group various model elements that are conceptually related.

Chapter 6, Events, Actions, and Activities, begins the exploration of the dynamic side of the UML in terms of the various ways by which object behavior is initiated, the UML's *action language* (which defines the individual, primitive functions that serve as the lowest level of behavior specification), and activities, which provide control and data sequencing constraints among actions as well as nested structuring mechanisms for control and scope.

Chapter 7, State Machines, discusses the UML constructs that you can use to model discrete object behavior in terms of the states that an object can reside in and the transitions that can happen between those states.

Chapter 8, Interactions, discusses the various aspects of interactions. The focus is on the messages that pass back and forth between objects during system execution. The chapter also provides examples of the four types of interaction diagrams that UML 2.0 supports.

Chapter 9, Components, Deployment, and Higher-Level Modeling, focuses on the modeling of autonomous units within a system or subsystem that the modeler can use to define software systems of arbitrary size and complexity. The chapter also discusses the modeling of the deployment of those units.

Chapter 10, Profiles, Templates, and Information Flows, discusses topics that don't quite fit into the preceding chapters, yet are important elements of the UML. The focus is on profiles, which are stereotyped packages that contain elements customized for a particular domain or purpose, and templates, which provide ways to create families of model elements such as classes, packages, and collaborations.

The book also includes the following end matter:

- An appendix that describes the various stereotypes that are built in to the UML

- A glossary, which contains definitions for all the terms I introduce

- A bibliography, which lists all the books I mention

- A complete index

CHAPTER 1

Classes

LET'S BEGIN OUR LOOK AT THE DETAILS of the Unified Modeling Language (UML) by exploring how we do basic modeling of things and concepts in the real world.

Classes and Objects

A *class* is a collection of things or concepts that have the same characteristics. Each of these things or concepts is called an *object*.

An object that belongs to a particular class is often referred to as an *instance* of that class. You can think of a class as being an abstraction and an object as being the concrete manifestation of that abstraction.

The class is the most fundamental construct within the UML. Reasons why this is so include the following:

- Classes define the basic vocabulary of the system being modeled. Using a set of classes as the core glossary of a project tends to greatly facilitate understanding and agreement about the meanings of terms.

- Classes can serve as the foundation for data modeling. Unfortunately, there is no standard for mapping between a set of classes and a set of database tables, but people like Scott Ambler[1] are working to change that.

- Classes are usually the base from which visual modeling tools—such as Rational Rose XDE, Embarcadero Describe, and Sparx Systems' Enterprise Architect—generate code.

The most important characteristics that classes share are captured as attributes and operations. These terms are defined as follows:

- *Attributes* are named slots for data values that belong to the class. Different objects of a given class typically have at least some differences in the values of their attributes.

---

[1] Scott Ambler, *Agile Database Techniques: Effective Strategies for the Agile Software Developer* (New York, NY: John Wiley & Sons, 2003).

- *Operations* represent services that an object can request to affect behavior. (A *method* is an implementation of an operation; each operation of a given class is represented by at least one method within each of the objects belonging to that class.)

The standard UML notation for a class is a box with three compartments. The top compartment contains the name of the class, in boldface type; the middle compartment contains the attributes that belong to the class; and the bottom compartment contains the class's operations. See Figure 1-1.

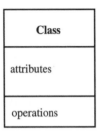

Figure 1-1. Class notation

You can, however, show a class without its attributes or its operations, or the name of the class can appear by itself (see Figure 1-2).

Figure 1-2. Alternate class notations

The level of detail you choose to show for your classes depends on who is reading the diagrams on which they appear. For example, a stakeholder who's focused on the "big picture" is probably interested only in the names of the classes, while a developer working at a more detailed level probably wants to see a full set of attributes and operations. You can also "mix and match" notations in a given context.

Figure 1-3 shows some examples of classes.

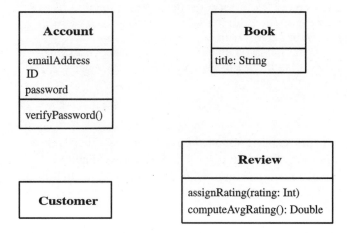

Figure 1-3. Sample classes

The names of the classes, attributes, and operations in Figure 1-3 adhere to conventions that aren't carved in stone but are in fairly wide use. These conventions are as follows:

- Class names are simple nouns or noun phrases. Each word is capitalized.

- Attribute names are also simple nouns or noun phrases. The first word is not capitalized, but subsequent words are. Acronyms tend to appear in all uppercase letters.

- Operation names are simple verbs. As with attributes, the first word is not capitalized and subsequent words are; acronyms tend to appear in all uppercase letters here as well.

Note that all words in class, attribute, and operation names are generally run together, as shown in Figure 1-3.

Whether you choose these simple conventions—or more elaborate ones— the naming of classes, attributes, and operations should be consistent with the language or platform that you're using or with your company-specific coding standards.

NOTE   The `title` attribute of the Book class has an associated data type (String), whereas the other three attributes in the figure (`emailAddress`, `ID`, and `password`) don't have types. Note also that each of the three operations (`verifyPassword`, `assignRating`, and `computeAvgRating`) has a different appearance. There are various kinds of details that you can attach to attributes and operations. These are explored in the section "Attribute and Operation Details," later in this chapter.

It's often desirable to define explicit *responsibilities* for a class. These represent the obligations that one class has with regard to other classes. Figure 1-4 shows how you can use an extra compartment within a UML class box to indicate responsibilities for a class.

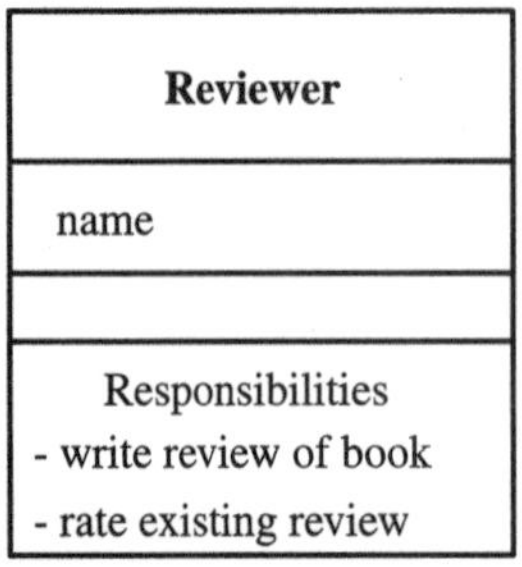

Figure 1-4. Class responsibilities

The idea of assigning responsibilities to classes is at the center of Class-Responsibility-Collaboration (CRC) cards.[2] This idea is also central to Responsibility-Driven Design.[3]

As development proceeds, responsibilities tend to get explicitly addressed by operations as classes get refined. So, you shouldn't be surprised if you don't see the responsibility compartment in later versions of models that include class boxes.

NOTE   You can also extend a class box with other compartments that contain whatever information you want to see. You find examples of these other compartments later in the book.

---

[2] David Bellin and Susan Suchman Simone, *The CRC Card Book* (Boston, MA: Addison-Wesley, 1997).

[3] Rebecca Wirfs-Brock, Brian Wilkerson, and Lauren Wiener, *Designing Object-Oriented Software* (Englewood Cliffs, NJ: Prentice-Hall, 1990).

The notation for an object takes the same basic form as that for a class. There are three differences between the notations, as follows:

- Within the top compartment of the class box, the name of the class to which the object belongs appears after a colon. The object may have a name, which appears before the colon, or it may be anonymous, in which case nothing appears before the colon.

- The contents of the top compartment are underlined for an object.

- Each attribute defined for the given class has a specific value for each object that belongs to that class.

Figure 1-5 shows the notation for both a named object (left) and an anonymous object (right).

Figure 1-5. UML object notation

Classes appear primarily on class diagrams; objects appear primarily on object diagrams. Chapter 3 describes both of these diagrams.

Discovering Classes

A simple yet effective way to discover classes uses a technique variously known as *noun/verb analysis* and *grammatical inspection.* This involves poring through high-level requirements documents, marketing materials, and other materials that provide insight into the problem domain (in other words, the arena defined by the problem that the new system is supposed to solve). See *Use Case Driven Object Modeling with UML*[4] for an example of how to perform grammatical inspection using a set of text requirements.

Many people use rapid prototyping as a device for exploring requirements with users. Let's see how we might use a prototype HTML page for an Internet bookstore to discover a small subset of the classes we'll need in modeling the bookstore as a whole. We start with a page that displays the details of a particular book.

---

[4] Doug Rosenberg with Kendall Scott, *Use Case Driven Object Modeling with UML* (Boston, MA: Addison-Wesley, 1999).

A quick mental review of the page reveals the following obvious candidates for classes:

- There's a Book, of course, and at least one Author.

- There's a Publisher.

- There may be one or more Reviews of the Book. These Reviews fall into one of two categories: EditorialReviews and CustomerReviews. (You see how to make this distinction in Chapter 2.) Each Review has a Reviewer associated with it.

If we move ahead and envision the viewer of this page purchasing the Book, the following other potential classes come into view:

- The viewer becomes a Customer, with an associated Account.

- The Book becomes part of an Order.

- The Order has to have BillingInformation and ShippingInformation in order for the bookstore to get paid and to ship the book.

Analyzing a little more deeply reveals the need for the following two other classes:

- A Book can have more than one Author, as I've noted, but an Author can have more than one Book, too. In the interest of avoiding many-to-many relationships, we need a BookAndAuthor class. (You see how to represent this class in Chapter 2.)

- The bookstore uses various shipping companies, so there needs to be a Shipper class.

The result, then, is the following set of nouns and noun phrases:

- Account

- Author

- BillingInfo

- Book

- BookAndAuthor

- Customer

- CustomerReview

- EditorialReview

- Order

- Publisher

- Review

- Reviewer

- Shipper

- ShippingInfo

> **NOTE**   This example is representative of a fundamentally sound idea: Find as many nouns and noun phrases as possible to start, and only analyze, refine, and expand the list later. Regardless of how you go about it, though, discovering classes is an excellent way to get your modeling off to a good start.

Attribute and Operation Details

The UML offers a variety of constructs that allow you to specify details for attributes and operations. These constructs are discussed in the following subsections.

Visibility

Encapsulation is the principle of data hiding: An object hides its data from the rest of the world and only lets outsiders manipulate that data by way of calls to the object's methods. The degree to which the elements of a class are encapsulated within that class depends on the level of visibility that's been assigned to the elements. The *visibility* of an attribute or an operation specifies whether objects that belong to other classes can "see" that attribute or operation.

The UML supports the following four levels of visibility:

- **Package visibility** (shown with a tilde [~]) means that objects belonging to any class in the same package as the given class can see and use the given class it. (Packages are discussed in Chapter 5.)

- **Public visibility** (+) means that objects belonging to any class can use the given attribute or operation.

- **Protected visibility** (#) means that only objects that belong to subclasses of the given class (at any level below that class) can use the attribute or operation. (Subclasses are discussed in Chapter 2.)

- **Private visibility** (–) means that only objects belonging to the class itself can use the attribute or operation.

Figure 1-6 shows visibility adornments on example attributes and operations.

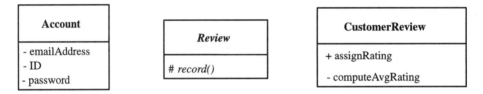

Figure 1-6. Visibility

The assignRating operation of the CustomerReview class is public, which means that objects of any other class can use it. The record operation of Review is protected, so CustomerReview objects and EditorialReview objects can use it, and objects of any subclasses of those two classes would be able to use it as well, but objects of classes outside that hierarchy cannot use record. The emailAddress, ID, and password attributes of Account are private: Only Account objects have access to these attributes. Similarly, CustomerReview objects are the only ones that can use the computeAvgRating operation.

> **NOTE**   The Review class and its record operation are abstract. Abstract classes and operations, which appear in italics to differentiate them from "concrete" classes and operations, are discussed in the section "Abstract Classes," later in this chapter.

More About Attributes

The full form of a UML attribute declaration is as follows:

[*visibility*] [*/*] *name* [*: type*] [*multiplicity*] [*= default*] [*{property-string}*]

The rectangular brackets surround optional items, which means that only the name is required. However, UML diagrams generally show details about attributes once serious design work commences on a project.

Visibility was discussed in the previous section. A forward slash appearing before the name of the attribute means that a value of the attribute can be derived from the values of one or more other attributes. For instance, if an object has an attribute named dateOfBirth and another attribute named age, the value of the latter attribute could be computed based on the value of the former.

Examples of built-in attribute data types include Double, Int (short for Integer), and String (which appeared in Figure 1-3). An attribute type can also be a user-defined type or the name of a class.

Multiplicity indicates how many of one thing can exist relative to another thing. A multiplicity expression can take several forms, including the following:

- A fixed value (such as 1 or 3)

- An asterisk (*), which means "many"

- A range of values, expressed as lower..upper (for instance, 0..1 or 3..*)

- A set of values (for example, [1, 3, 5, 7])

A multiplicity value on an attribute indicates how many instances of that attribute are present for each instance of the class. The multiplicity of an attribute appears between square brackets after the attribute name.

A default value of an attribute for a class means that each instance of that class has that initial value for the given attribute.

The most important property you can attach to an attribute declaration is readOnly, which indicates that you can add possible values for the attribute, but you can't change existing values.

Figure 1-7 shows details of some of the attributes of an example class.

Account
emailAddress [1..3] ID: String {readOnly} password = 1234

Figure 1-7. Attribute details

> **NOTE** An object belonging to the Account class can have from one to three email addresses. Each Account object has an ID that can't be deleted; you might think of this as being the equivalent of the key within a database table. And, there's an initial value for an Account object's password, which the Customer is likely to change but which is useful in case the Customer forgets to define a password when he or she sets up an Account.

More About Operations

The full form of a UML operation declaration is as follows:

`[visibility] name [(parameter-list)] [{property-string}]`

As with attributes, the rectangular brackets surround optional items.

A discussion of visibility appeared earlier in this chapter. The parameters of an operation, which appear in a list separated by commas, represent the data provided by the caller of the operation, the data that the operation returns to the caller, or both. The full form of a parameter declaration is as follows:

`[direction] name : type [multiplicity] [= default-value]`

A parameter can have one of the following three directions:

- in (The operation can't modify the parameter, so the caller doesn't need to see it again.)

- out (The operation sets or changes the value of the parameter and returns it to the caller.)

- inout (The operation uses the value of the parameter and may change the value; the caller expects to see an inout parameter again.)

Types work the same way for parameters as they do for attributes. See the section "More About Attributes," earlier in this chapter, for a discussion of multiplicity. A default value of a parameter for an operation means that each call to that operation includes that value for the given parameter.

One property that you can attach to an operation declaration is isQuery, which indicates that the operation doesn't change the values of any attributes. There are three other properties that relate to *concurrency*, which has to do with how a method that implements a given operation responds in the context of multiple threads of activity. The three possible concurrency values are as follows:

- concurrent (Multiple method calls, from multiple threads, may come in simultaneously to the method, and these calls can all proceed concurrently.)

- guarded (Multiple calls may come in simultaneously, but only one can proceed at a time.)

- sequential (Only one call may come in at a time.)

Figure 1-8 shows some details of operations belonging to an example class.

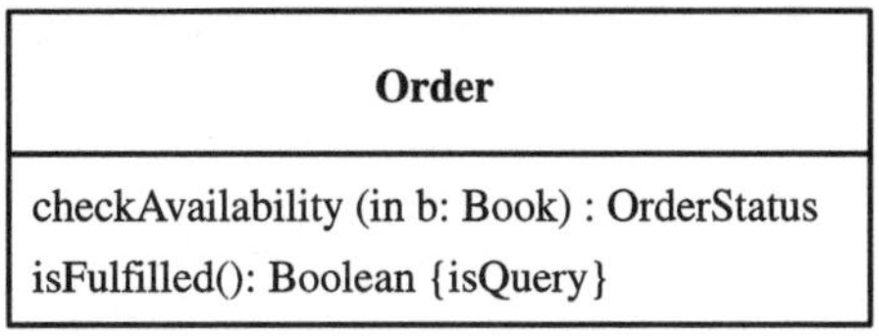

Order
checkAvailability (in b: Book) : OrderStatus isFulfilled(): Boolean {isQuery}

Figure 1-8. Operation details

The checkAvailability operation receives a Book object (see Figure 1-3) and returns a value of the user-defined type OrderStatus. The isFulfilled operation is a query that returns True if everything the customer ordered is in place or False otherwise.

You can add precision to your modeling of operations by indicating *constraints,* which specify conditions that must hold true in a given context. You show a constraint as a Boolean expression between curly brackets.

> **NOTE** The UML defines a separate language, called the Object Constraint Language (OCL), that you can use to specify constraints. Using the OCL enables you to reach a certain level of rigor in your modeling without side effects. In other words, the evaluation of OCL expressions can't alter the state of the executing system. See *The Object Constraint Language*[5] for more information about the OCL.

Two kinds of constraints are of particular interest in the context of operations: preconditions and postconditions.

---

[5] Jos Warmer and Anneke Klempe, *The Object Constraint Language: Precise Modeling with UML* (Boston, MA: Addison-Wesley, 1998).

A *precondition* specifies a condition that must hold true before an operation starts executing. Figure 1-9 shows an example of a precondition contained within a *note,* which you can use to record comments about a model without affecting the content of the model.

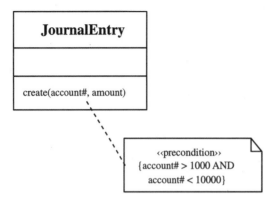

Figure 1-9. Precondition

Note that the triangular brackets (called *guillemets*) around the word *precondition* indicate the presence of a *stereotype.* This is a mechanism for building a modeling construct that isn't identified in the core UML but that's similar to things that are part of the core. Stereotypes of various kinds appear throughout this book; some of them are built in to the UML, while others are user defined.

A *postcondition* specifies a condition that must hold true before an operation starts executing. Figure 1-10 shows an example of a postcondition.

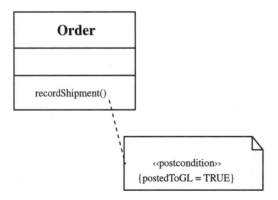

Figure 1-10. Postcondition

You can also specify which exceptions a given operation raises. One way to do this is to create a note with «exception» at the top followed by a list of exception types relevant to the operation. (You read about other ways to specify exceptions in Chapter 6.)

Abstract Classes

An *abstract class* is a class that can't have any instances.

Abstract classes are generally designed to capture operations that subclasses inherit. The idea is that the operations defined for an abstract class are relatively general, and each class that inherits these operations refines and expands upon them. (You explore inheritance in Chapter 2.)

In UML notation, the name of an abstract class appears in italics (see Figure 1-11).

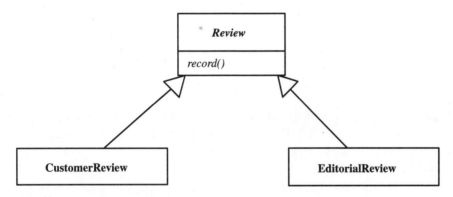

Figure 1-11. Abstract class

NOTE   Figure 1-11 adds an abstract operation, record, to the Review class. CustomerReview and EditorialReview both inherit this operation, but the operation works differently in the context of each class.

You can also use an «abstract» stereotype for readers of the model who might not realize the significance of the italics.

Active Classes

An *active class* is a class that represents an independent flow of control, such as a process or a thread.

The class box for an active class has thin vertical bars just inside the borders, as shown in Figure 1-12.

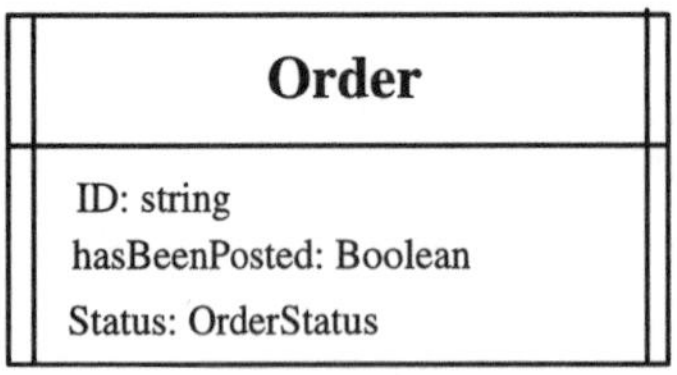

Order
ID: string hasBeenPosted: Boolean Status: OrderStatus

Figure 1-12. Active class

The instances of an active class are called *active objects.*

Interfaces, Ports, and Connectors

An *interface* is a collection of operations that represent services offered by a class or a component. (A discussion of components appears in Chapter 9.) By definition, all of these operations have public visibility. (See the section "Visibility," earlier in this chapter.)

One of the key tenets of object orientation is the separation of an interface from the details of how the exposed operations are implemented as methods. The interface specifies something like a contract that a class must adhere to; the class *realizes* (or provides a *realization* for) one or more interfaces.

The UML defines two kinds of interfaces: provided interfaces and required interfaces.

Provided interfaces are interfaces that a class provides to potential clients for the operations that it offers (such as objects belonging to other classes). There are two ways to show a provided interface. One way is called "lollipop" notation: The interface is a circle attached to the class box with a straight line. The other way involves defining the interface using a class box and the built-in «interface» stereotype, and then drawing a dashed line with a triangle at the end that has the interface.

Figure 1-13 shows two examples of provided interfaces, using both notations.

Figure 1-13. Provided interfaces

Setting up a Password Handler interface to the Account class provides the flexibility to use different encryption algorithms in the implementation of the operation that stores customer passwords. Along the same lines, the Inventory Handler interface allows elements of the system to interact with objects belonging to the Inventory class without having to know whether the inventory system uses FIFO (first in, first out), LIFO (last in, first out), or some other method of handling inventory.

Required interfaces are interfaces that a class needs to fulfill its duties. The symbol for a required interface is a half-circle, as shown in Figure 1-14.

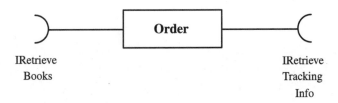

Figure 1-14. Required interfaces

Instances of the Order class use Retrieve Books in fulfilling the given order and Retrieve Tracking Info if the Customer that placed the order wants to track the order's shipping history. (More detail about these interfaces appears in the following paragraphs.)

You can also show one class providing an interface that another class requires, using "ball and socket" notation, where the ball represents the provided interface and the socket indicates the required interface. Figure 1-15 shows an example.

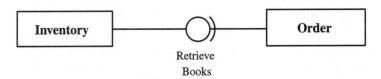

Figure 1-15. Provided/required interface

The Inventory class provides the Retrieve Books interface that the Order class requires, as shown in Figure 1-14.

A *port* specifies a distinct interaction point between a class and its environment. Ports group provided interfaces and/or required interfaces in two ways. They serve as focal points through which requests can be made to invoke the operations that the class makes available. They also serve as gateways for calls that the class makes to operations offered by other classes.

A port appears as a small square on the boundary of the class box. Interfaces are connected to a port via *connectors,* which are simple straight lines. Figure 1-16 shows two example ports, one with a name and one without.

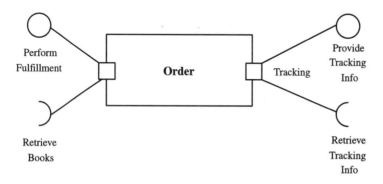

Figure 1-16. Ports and connectors

An instance of the Order class receives a request to fulfill the actual order that the instance represents via the Perform Fulfillment interface. The Order instance uses the Retrieve Books interface in meeting this request. After the given order is shipped, the associated Customer may request tracking information via the Provide Tracking Info interface. The Order instance, in turn, uses the Retrieve Tracking Info interface to acquire the necessary information to return to the Customer.

Internal Class Structure

The behavior of a class can be partly or fully described by a set of objects that the class references and/or owns. Each of these objects is called a *property* of the class.

Figure 1-17 shows that the GeneralLedger class has three properties: Posting is owned by composition, while PostingRule is "owned" by aggregation. (See the section "Aggregation" in Chapter 2 for definitions of these terms.)

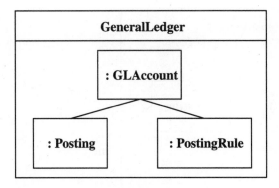

Figure 1-17. Properties

A GLAccount instance owns the Postings made to it, which is why that relationship is a composition. A PostingRule, on the other hand, exists independent of any particular GLAccount instance, which is why that relationship is an aggregation.

An object that is contained by composition is also referred to as a *part*. Figure 1-18 shows the GeneralLedger class as having two parts.

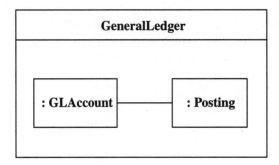

Figure 1-18. Parts

Note that the notation for a part can also contain a multiplicity value (see the section "More About Attributes," earlier in this chapter). This value can appear in the upper-right corner of the object box or in square brackets next to the object name.

Ports can be connected to parts within classes, as shown in Figure 1-19 (see the section "Interfaces, Ports, and Connectors," earlier in this chapter). Each part provides the functionality that external entities request via the associated port.

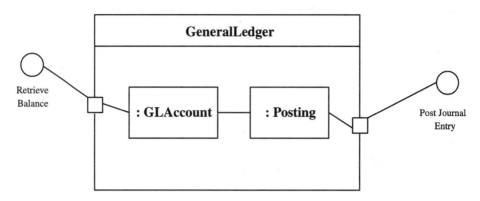

Figure 1-19. Ports and parts

Anyone in the Accounting department who needs the current balance of a given GLAccount accesses that instance via the Retrieve Balance interface. The software that handles the posting of journal entries goes through the Post Journal Entry interface in order to create an instance of the Posting class, which posts to a particular GLAccount.

Figure 1-19 is an example of a *composite structure diagram.* This type of diagram shows the internal structure of a class or a collaboration (see the next section, "Collaborations").

A special kind of port, called a *behavior port,* passes requests for specific behavior to the instance of the given class itself, rather than to any instances that the class may contain. Figure 1-20 shows the symbol for a behavior port.

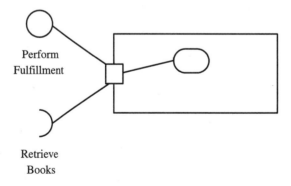

Figure 1-20. Behavior port

Collaborations

A *collaboration* is a description of a named structure of classes. Instances of these classes each perform some specialized function (in other words, each serves a particular role). Taken together, these instances collectively accomplish some desired functionality that's greater than the sum of the parts.

The name of a collaboration should be a simple noun phrase that communicates the essence of what the collaboration does. The symbol for a collaboration is an ellipse with a dashed outline. Figure 1-21 shows two example collaborations.

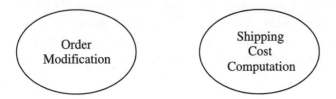

Figure 1-21. Collaborations

You can also show the internal structure (in terms of instances) of a collaboration, as shown in Figure 1-22. The lines between instances represent connectors—and thus communication paths.

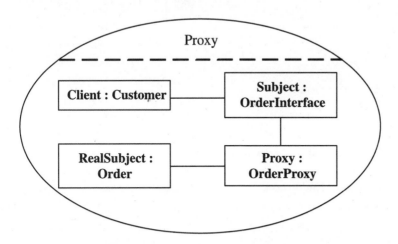

Figure 1-22. Collaboration with internal structure

The Proxy collaboration is actually an example of a design pattern.[6] The names before the colons are those that the pattern specifies; the names after the colons are names, defined by the modeler, for entities that are playing the specified roles.

A Customer retrieving information about his or her Order is presented with an OrderInterface in the form of an HTML page. This interface provides the Customer with an OrderProxy that stands in for the actual Order instance. This is necessary because Order instances are responsible for directing system processes (see the section "Active Classes," earlier in this chapter) and thus shouldn't be directly accessible by Customers. The OrderProxy does access the Order as necessary for information, without disrupting system operations.

Figure 1-22 is another example of a composite structure diagram.

A *collaboration occurrence* is the application of the pattern described by a particular collaboration to a specific situation that involves specific classes or instances playing the roles of that collaboration.

The notation for a collaboration occurrence is comparable to that of an object: the name of the occurrence, a colon, and the name of the collaboration. If the occurrence represents some behavior offered by a class, the occurrence is connected with the class using a *represents* dependency. Figure 1-23 shows an example of this dependency.

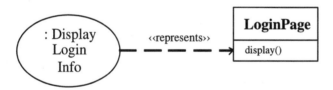

Figure 1-23. Collaboration occurrence

Other Stereotypes on Classes

There are other built-in stereotypes that may prove useful in helping you define classes. These stereotypes are as follows:

- Two stereotypes differentiate between primary and secondary logic or control flow. The «focus» stereotype signifies that a class provides primary logic; the «auxiliary» stereotype signifies that a class supports one or more «focus» classes.

---

[6] Erich Gamma, Richard Helm, Ralph Johnson, and John Vlissides, *Design Patterns: Elements of Reusable Object-Oriented Software* (Boston, MA: Addison-Wesley, 1995). Note that this group of authors is often referred to as the "Gang of Four."

Within Figure 1-24, the GLReport class contains logic for formatting and printing a report that contains information provided by the General Ledger class.

Figure 1-24. Auxiliary and focus stereotypes

- Three stereotypes signify sets of values that have no identities and that can't be changed by operations.

The «dataType» stereotype is the "parent" stereotype. Figure 1-25 shows two examples of user-defined data types.

Figure 1-25. Data types

The «enumeration» stereotype signifies an ordered list of literals. Figure 1-26 shows an example of a user-defined enumeration.

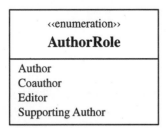

Figure 1-26. Enumeration

This enumeration might be a useful alternative to the BookAndAuthor class that appeared earlier in the chapter. If that class weren't present, it's likely that the Author class will have an AuthorRole attribute.

The «primitive» stereotype signifies a data type built in to the UML. There are four primitive types: Boolean, Int, String, and UnlimitedNatural. (The latter is equivalent to "real.")

- The «utility» stereotype signifies that the attributes and operations that belong to a class all have class scope—in other words, the attributes and operations define data, or operate on data, for the class as a whole, as there are no instances of the class.

- Two stereotypes offer a way to differentiate classes when you start modeling implementation.

  The «specification» stereotype signifies that a class specifies the characteristics of a set of objects without defining the physical implementation of those objects.

  The «implementationClass» stereotype signifies that a class provides a static physical implementation of its objects. An implementation class is usually associated with a static class within a programming language, such as C++.

- You can use «stereotype» itself as a stereotype to signify that a class is itself a stereotype that can be applied to other elements of your model.

  Within Figure 1-27, the class HTMLPage also serves as a stereotype that applies to FormPage and InformationalPage.

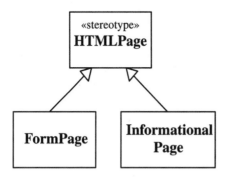

Figure 1-27. Stereotype as stereotype

- The «metaclass» stereotype signifies that all instances of a class are themselves classes. For example, Class is the metaclass of classes you've seen to this point, such as HTMLPage. This is useful if you're exploring more expansive ways to expand the UML. Unfortunately, metamodeling is beyond the scope of this book.

Looking Ahead

In Chapter 2, you look at the various kinds of relationships in which classes can be involved. The combination of classes and relationships forms the heart of the UML's structural modeling constructs.

CHAPTER 2

Class Relationships

CLASSES, BY THEMSELVES, AREN'T PARTICULARLY USEFUL. It's the relationships among classes that provide the foundation for the structure of a new system. The following sections explore how you use the UML to illustrate various kinds of class relationships.

Associations

An *association* is a simple structural connection between classes.

You might think of an association as representing a "peer" relationship. (You look at other kinds of relationships that involve "parents" and "children," and "parts" and "the whole," later in the chapter.) Instances of classes involved in an association will most likely be communicating with each other at program execution time, but all we're concerned with here is the fact that these instances have some attachment to each other. (By the way, an instance of an association—in other words, a structural connection between objects—is called a *link*.)

There are two basic kinds of associations: binary associations and n-ary associations.

A *binary association*, which exists between two classes, appears as a straight line that connects them. Figure 2-1 shows some example associations between classes.

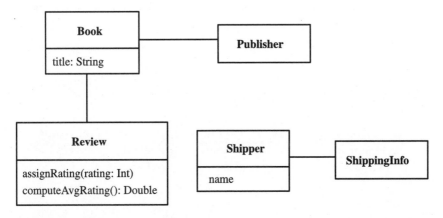

Figure 2-1. Binary associations

An *n-ary association,* which exists among three or more classes, appears as a set of lines connected to a central diamond, as shown in Figure 2-2.

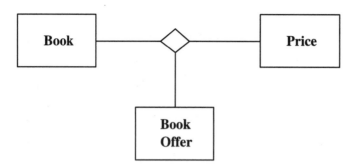

Figure 2-2. N-ary association

The n-ary association is considered something of an advanced modeling construct; you're much more likely to see—and use—plain binary associations in your models.

An association is assumed to be bidirectional, which means that you can navigate from either class to the other one. However, you can specify that navigation can only occur from one class to another by using a feathered arrow, as shown in Figure 2-3.

Figure 2-3. One-way navigation between classes

Establishing the navigation arrow on this association means that a Customer has access to his or her Password, but no one can in turn use a Password to identify a Customer.

You can add several kinds of details, or *adornments,* to an association. These adornments include the following:

• An association can have a name that indicates the nature of the relationship. If a name is present, there can also be a triangle that points in the direction in which you should read the name. See Figure 2-4.

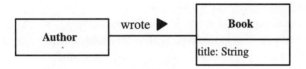

Figure 2-4. Named association

- An association can contain *roles,* which are the faces that classes present to other classes. As shown in Figure 2-5, roles generally appear in pairs.

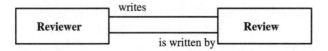

Figure 2-5. Association roles

You read an association with role names from a class to the role immediately next to it to the class on the other side of the association. In other words, you would read this association in one direction as "Reviewer writes Review" and in the other direction as "Review is written by Reviewer."

A class can play the same role or different roles within different associations.

- An association can show *multiplicity.* See the section "More About Attributes" in Chapter 1 for more on this topic. Figure 2-6 shows two examples of association multiplicity.

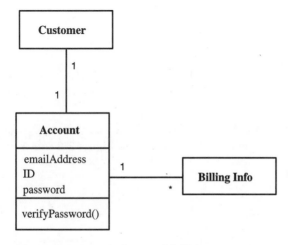

Figure 2-6. Association multiplicity

When an association has multiplicities attached to it, you read from a class to the value next to the *other* class, across the association. So, in Figure 2-6, one Account can be associated with many Billing Info objects, but each Billing Info object is associated with only one Account.

Aggregation

An *aggregation* is a special kind of association—a "whole/part" relationship within which one or more classes are parts of a larger whole. A class can be aggregated to one or more other classes.

Using aggregation is an excellent way to establish a "pecking order" of complexity, with more complex classes aggregating less complex ones. For a system of any size, doing this can only help viewers of your models more easily understand the concepts that are important to them while enabling them to ignore concepts expressed at lower levels of detail.

An aggregation appears as a line with an open diamond at one end. The class next to the diamond is the *whole* class; the class at the other end of the line is the *part* class. See Figure 2-7.

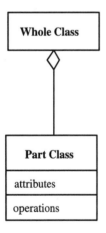

Figure 2-7. Aggregation notation

If a given class aggregates more than one class, you can show each aggregation using a separate line, or you can consolidate the lines. Figure 2-8 shows both variations.

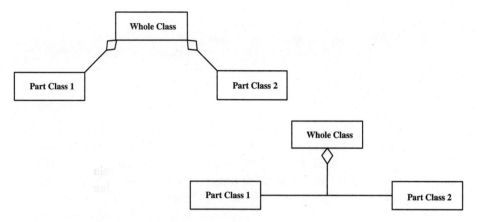

Figure 2-8. Aggregating multiple classes

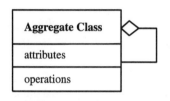

Figure 2-9. Self-aggregation

A class can also aggregate itself, as shown in Figure 2-9.

This self-aggregation construct is useful in situations such as those that involve "rollups" for reporting purposes. (A *rollup* is a consolidation of information expressed at one or more particular levels of detail into a higher level of detail.)

Figure 2-10 shows some example aggregations.

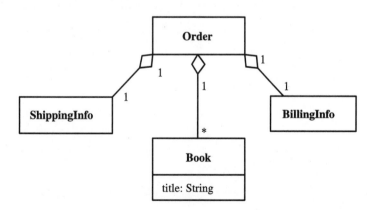

Figure 2-10. Aggregations

> **NOTE**   Multiplicities now appear on each aggregation relationship. If an aggregation doesn't show multiplicity values, the default is many (*) parts and one whole.

Figure 2-10 shows that an instance of the Order class aggregates one each of instances of the ShippingInfo and BillingInfo classes and one or more instances of the Book class. An important property of aggregation is that the aggregated classes are still basically independent of the aggregating class. In other words, when a particular Order goes away (because it's been archived, for example), the ShippingInfo and BillingInfo instances that were aggregated to that Order are still present in the system. (The Book instance, of course, is gone.)

Composition is a "strong" form of aggregation. There are two differences between composition and regular aggregation, as follows:

- Within a composition relationship, the whole and the parts have coincident lifetimes. This means that if a particular instance of the whole is destroyed, so are the instances of the parts.

- A class can only belong to one composition relationship at a time as a part.

Figure 2-11 shows an example of a composition relationship.

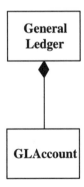

Figure 2-11. Composition

This relationship specifies that a GLAccount in a composition relationship with a particular GeneralLedger is destroyed when that GeneralLedger is destroyed.

Composition versus aggregation is generally an issue that comes up during activities such as physical database design. It's not generally a distinction that you need to worry about at, say, the analysis level.

Generalization

Generalization refers to a relationship between a general class (the *superclass* or *parent*) and a more specific version of that class (the *subclass* or *child*). You can think of the subclass as being a "kind of" the superclass.

A generalization appears as a line with an open triangle at one end. The class next to the triangle is the parent/superclass; the class at the other end of the line is the child/subclass. See Figure 2-12.

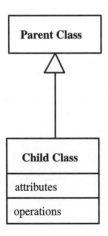

Figure 2-12. Generalization notation

If a given class has more than one child/subclass, you can show each generalization using a separate line, or you can consolidate the lines, as with aggregation. Figure 2-13 shows both variations.

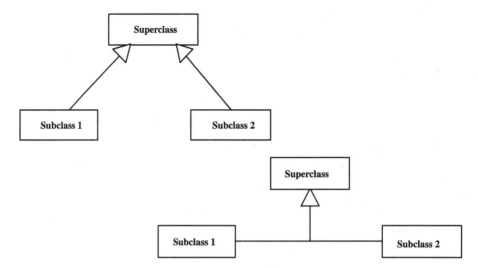

Figure 2-13. Generalizing multiple classes

Figure 2-14 shows a sample generalization.

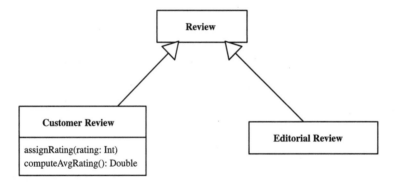

Figure 2-14. Generalization

Note the change between Figure 2-14 and Figure 1-3 (see Chapter 1): The operations that used to belong to the Review class have been "pushed down" into Customer Review. This is because these methods don't apply to the new Editorial Review class. This is a good example of how the subclass, Customer Review, specializes the more general superclass, Review.

We've only looked at "single" inheritance to this point, but the UML also offers a way to model multiple inheritance—in other words, generalizations within which a class is a child of two or more parents. The basic notation is the same; the diagrams just get a little harder to read. Multiple inheritance is something of a tricky subject that's outside the scope of this book, except as referenced in the following paragraphs. (It's also something that some implementation platforms, such as .NET, and languages, such as C#, don't support.)

You can use a *generalization set* to define partitions for the subclasses of a particular class (the superclass). The superclass acts as the *powertype* for the generalization set, which means that the instances of that superclass are also subclasses of another class.

Within Figure 2-15, PaymentType serves as a powertype on Payment.

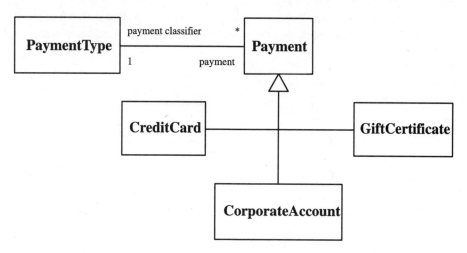

Figure 2-15. Powertype

In other words, the instances of PaymentType include those named CreditCard, CorporateAccount, and GiftCertificate—each of which is, in turn, a subclass of Payment. Each of these classes forms its own generalization set; this provides the modeler with extra flexibility in defining behavior associated with each subclass.

The UML offers the following four constraints (see the section "More About Operations" in Chapter 1), which you can use in conjunction with generalization sets:

- The {incomplete} constraint means that not all children have been specified for a given generalization set and that more can be specified.

- The {complete} constraint means that all children have been specified for a given generalization set and that no more can be specified.

- The {disjoint} constraint means that given multiple inheritance, no object can be an instance of more than one child within the generalization set.

- The {overlapping} constraint means that given multiple inheritance, an object can be an instance of more than one child within the generalization set.

Dependencies

A *dependency* is a "using" relationship within which a change in one thing (such as a class) may affect another thing (for instance, another class). The dependent element is called the *client* or *source;* the independent element is called the *supplier* or *target.*

A dependency involving two classes appears as a dashed line with a feathered arrow pointing at the supplier. Figure 2-16 shows an example of a dependency.

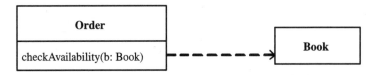

Figure 2-16. Dependency

If the definition of the Book class changes, the way that the checkAvailability function works may have to change as well.

The UML defines a number of stereotypes that apply to dependencies. These are explored in the following subsections.

Usage Dependencies

A *usage* dependency is one in which the client requires the presence of the supplier for its correct functioning or implementation.

You model a generic usage dependency using the «use» stereotype. Figure 2-17 shows that instances of the Order class require instances of the OrderItem class in order to function properly.

Figure 2-17. Usage dependency

The UML defines the following five types of usage dependencies:

- A *call* dependency («call») signifies that the source operation invokes the target operation.

- A *create* dependency («create») signifies that the source class creates one or more instances of the target class.

  Within Figure 2-18, an instance of the Order class creates one more instances of the JournalEntry class.

Figure 2-18. Create dependency

- An *instantiation* dependency («instantiate») signifies that one or more methods belonging to instances of the source class create instances of the target class.

  Within Figure 2-19, a method belonging to an instance of the HTMLPageHandler class creates an instance of the LoginPage class.

Figure 2-19. Instantiation

- A *responsibility* dependency («responsibility») signifies that the client has some kind of obligation to the supplier.

- A *send* dependency («send») signifies that instances of the source class send signals to instances of the target class. (Signals are discussed in Chapter 6.)

Abstraction Dependencies

An *abstraction* dependency is one in which the client is at one level of abstraction and the supplier is at a different level.

You model a generic usage dependency using the «abstraction» stereotype. Figure 2-20 shows that the SShoppingCart class is more concrete than the

ShoppingCart class. (A *session bean* is a type of EnterpriseJava Bean [EJB]. See *Mastering Enterprise JavaBeans*[1] for more information about EJBs.)

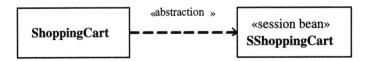

Figure 2-20. Abstraction dependency

The UML defines the following five types of abstraction dependencies:

- A *derivation* dependency («derive») signifies that the client can be computed or inferred from the supplier.

Within Figure 2-21, you can derive the association between Account and Order by navigating from Account to BillingInfo to Order.

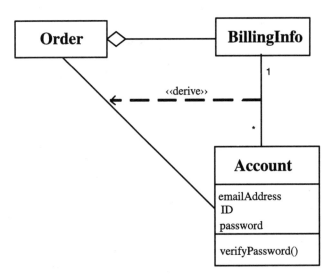

Figure 2-21. Derivation dependency

---

[1] Ed Roman, *Mastering Enterprise JavaBeans (Second Edition)* (New York, NY: John Wiley & Sons, 2001).

- A *realization* dependency («realize») signifies that the supplier serves as the implementation of the client. (Note that in this context, "implementation" implies a more elaborate form of the client, not necessarily a physical implementation as, say, program code.)

Within Figure 2-22, the PhysicalOrder class "implements" the Order class. (See the section "Other Stereotypes on Classes" in Chapter 1 for a discussion of the «implementationClass» stereotype.)

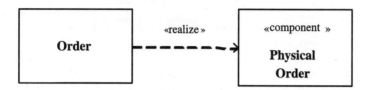

Figure 2-22. Realization dependency

Note the differences between this type of dependency and the type of realization discussed in Chapter 1 (see the section "Interfaces, Ports, and Connectors" in Chapter 1).

- A *refinement* dependency («refine») signifies that the supplier is at a lower level of abstraction than the client.

Within Figure 2-23, the Order class on the right is an active class that represents a refinement, at the design level, of the Order class on the left.

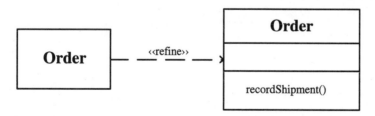

Figure 2-23. Refinement dependency

- A *trace* dependency («trace») signifies a conceptual connection among elements contained within different models.

Figure 2-24 shows that you can trace the LoginManager class, which probably belongs to the analysis-level model, to the SessionManager class, which probably belongs to a design-level model.

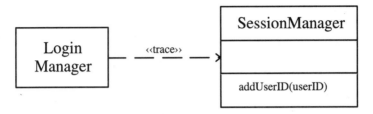

Figure 2-24. Trace dependency

- A *manifestation* dependency («manifest») signifies that a target artifact represents the concrete physical realization of one or more source classes. (Manifestations are discussed in Chapter 9.)

Permission and Substitution Dependencies

A *permission* dependency («permit») signifies that the supplier grants the client permission to access some or all of its constituent elements.

Within Figure 2-25, the Customer class grants the RecommendationEngine class access to its private attributes emailAddress and name.

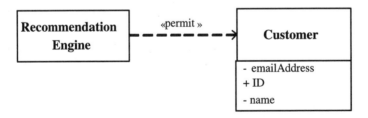

Figure 2-25. Permission dependency

A *substitution* dependency («substitute») signifies that the client will comply with the contract specified by the supplier at program execution time.

Within Figure 2-26, a more specific Login Page adheres to the basic framework within which a generic HTML Page works.

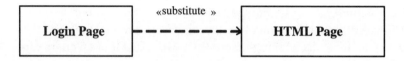

Figure 2-26. Substitution dependency

Association Classes

An *association class* is a cross between an association (see the section "Associations," earlier in this chapter) and a class (see Chapter 1).

You use an association class to model an association that has interesting characteristics of its own outside of the classes it connects. This construct also comes in handy when you have a many-to-many relationship that you'd like to break into a set of one-to-many relationships (as discussed in the section "Discovering Classes" in Chapter 1).

An association class itself appears as a regular class box. You indicate that it's an association class by connecting it to the association between the other two classes using a dashed line.

Figure 2-27 shows an example of an association class that was introduced in Chapter 1.

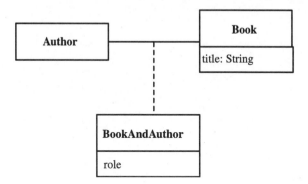

Figure 2-27. Association class

There would normally be a many-to-many relationship between Author and Book, because an Author may have written more than one Book and a Book may have more than one Author. The presence of the BookAndAuthor association class allows the pairing of one Author with one Book; the role attribute provides the option of stating whether the Author was the primary author, supporting author, or editor, for example.

Refer to the «enumeration» stereotype in the section "Other Stereotypes on Classes" in Chapter 1 for a discussion of an alternate way to model the `role` attribute. One of the most useful things about the UML is that it often offers various options for modeling a particular idea. Of course, this can also be a curse, but in general, it's the opinion of this author that having options is a good thing.

Looking Ahead

In the next chapter, you look at the UML diagrams that show combinations of classes and the relationships among them.

CHAPTER 3

Class and Object Diagrams

THIS CHAPTER FOCUSES ON THE UML STRUCTURAL diagrams that you use to capture the fundamental structure of your models at the class and object levels.

Class Diagrams

A *class diagram* focuses on a set of classes (see Chapter 1) and the structural relationships among them (see Chapter 2). It may also show interfaces (see the section "Interfaces, Ports, and Connectors" in Chapter 1).

The UML allows you to draw class diagrams that have varying levels of detail. One useful way to classify these diagrams involves three stages of a typical software development project: requirements, analysis, and design. These stages are discussed in the following sections.

Domain-Level Class Diagrams

A domain-level class diagram shows just the names of classes. The purpose of the diagram is to show part of the initial core vocabulary with which system modeling can proceed.

> **NOTE** Domain-level class diagrams are directly comparable to platform-independent models (PIMs) within Model-Driven Architecture (MDA). See *MDA Distilled*[1] for more information about MDA.

Figure 3-1 shows an example of a domain-level class diagram.

---

[1] Stephen J. Mellor, Kendall Scott, Axel Uhl, and Dirk Weise, *MDA Distilled: Principles of Model-Driven Architecture* (Boston, MA: Addison-Wesley, 2004).

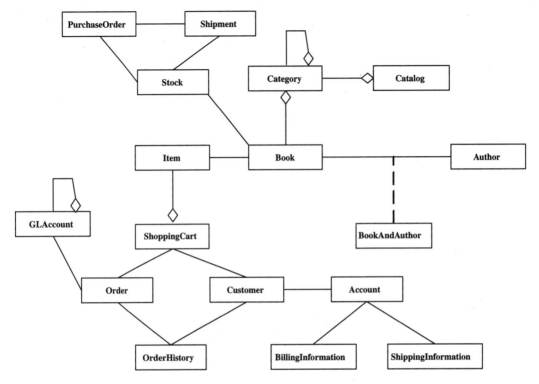

Figure 3-1. Domain-level class diagram

The layout of this diagram suggests five conceptual groupings of classes around which more expansive diagrams might center. Starting in the upper-left corner and moving clockwise, these groupings are as follows:

- PurchaseOrder, Shipment, and Stock

- Category, Catalog, Book, BookAndAuthor, and Author

- Customer, Account, BillingInfo, and ShippingInfo

- Item, ShoppingCart, Order, and OrderHistory

- GLAccount

In the meantime, this diagram provides a view of a useful cross section of the relevant starting classes.

Analysis-Level Class Diagrams

An analysis-level class diagram typically shows attributes; it may show other adornments such as multiplicity and role names as well. An analysis-level diagram, though, shouldn't have operations, because deciding where to put what operations definitely falls into the design arena. (See *Use Case Driven Object Modeling with UML*[2] for more on this topic.)

Figure 3-2 shows an example of an analysis-level class diagram.

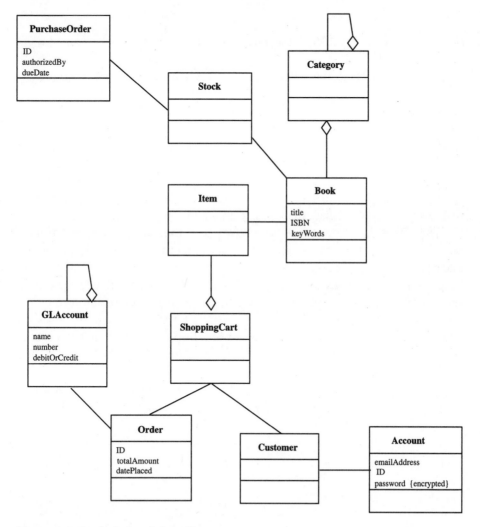

Figure 3-2. Analysis-level class diagram

---

[2] Doug Rosenberg with Kendall Scott, *Use Case Driven Object Modeling with UML* (Boston, MA: Addison-Wesley, 1999).

This is clearly an early version of this diagram, because there will certainly be more attributes for PurchaseOrder, GLAccount, Order, and Account, as well as a full set of attributes for the other classes. The point is that class diagrams evolve as knowledge of the domain being modeled grows.

Note the term {encrypted} that is attached to the Account attribute password. This is a user-defined constraint that indicates that the password undergoes encryption before being stored in the system. This is something of a design decision, but since this decision exists at the attribute level, it makes sense to go ahead and include the constraint on a class diagram at this level of precision.

Design-Level Class Diagrams

Once a project starts exploring design issues, class diagrams tend to be more varied. You can expand your classes using the full UML notation, or you can explore classes at a lower level of abstraction and continue to suppress the details (perhaps because those details are well-defined elsewhere).

One form of design-level class diagram is simply a more expansive version of an analysis-level diagram. Figure 3-3 expands the analysis-level class diagram of Figure 3-2 to show operations.

Figure 3-4 delves into some of the design-level classes that are connected with the ShoppingCart class that appears in Figure 3-1.

The new ShoppingCart class is an HTML page that contains a static form displaying the contents of the cart and a Java applet that allows the Customer to make changes to the contents of the cart. The CandidateOrder is a JavaServer Page that retrieves the essential information from the ShoppingCart page (the client) and stores the information on a server in a format suitable for further processing by the system. SShoppingCart is an Enterprise JavaBean that lives only until the Customer is done with his or her shopping cart, at which point the system creates a "persistent" EJB with the name EOrder; this is the form that the Customer's order takes going forward.

Figure 3-5 takes things another step closer to implementation by showing the classes that sit underneath the ShoppingCart class shown in Figure 3-4.

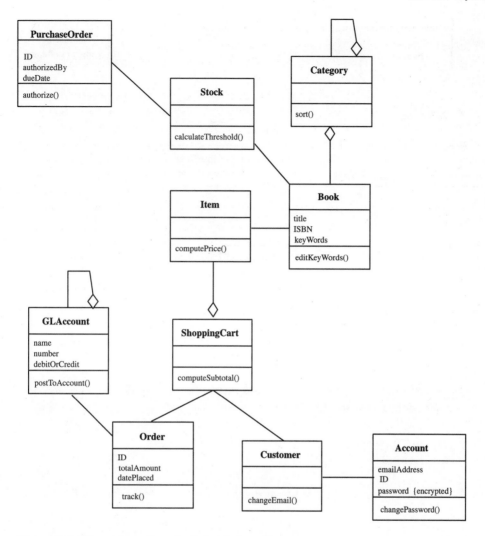

Figure 3-3. Expansion of analysis-level class diagram

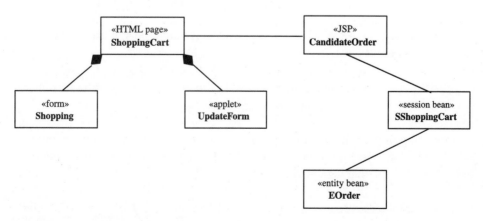

Figure 3-4. High-level design class diagram

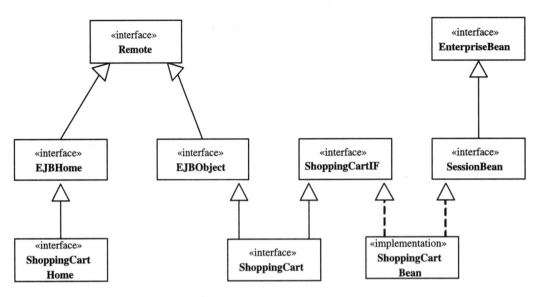

Figure 3-5. Low-level design class diagram

The elements of Figure 3-5 are as follows:

- Remote is the superclass of all interfaces through which clients have remote access to EJBs.

- EnterpriseBean is the superclass of EntityBean (not shown) and SessionBean.

- EJBHome defines operations such as create and remove for an EJB.

- EJBObject defines operations for accessing an EJB's data.

- ShoppingCartIF contains the user-defined operations for our EJB.

- SessionBean is a form of EJB that lives only while the system's session with the client is alive.

- ShoppingCartHome is the interface to the "factory" that creates instances of our EJB.

- ShoppingCart is the interface to our EJB. It offers the operations defined by both EJBObject and ShoppingCartIF, via multiple inheritance (see the section "Generalization" in Chapter 2).

- ShoppingCartBean implements the operations that ShoppingCartIF offers.

Figure 3-5, which is adapted from a diagram in *The Art of Objects*,[3] can serve as a diagram of a pattern in that everywhere ShoppingCart appears, you can simply plug in the name of another design-level class that involves EJBs. One idea, then, is to replace ShoppingCart with a generic class name and then refer to the resulting diagram from various other diagrams as appropriate.

Object Diagrams

An *object diagram* shows a set of objects, and the relationships among them, at a particular point in time during the execution of the system. Figure 3-6 shows an example of an object diagram.

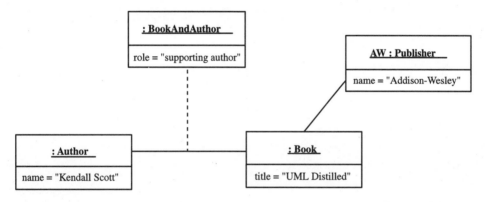

Figure 3-6. Object diagram

Most people use object diagrams sparingly, if at all. They're mostly good for capturing snapshots of particular situations during program execution when it's important to see the relationships of a set of object attributes.

Looking Ahead

In the next chapter, you start exploring how to use the UML to model the dynamic side of systems—in other words, user and system behavior.

---

[3] Yun-Tung Lau, *The Art of Objects: Object-Oriented Design and Architecture* (Boston, MA: Addison-Wesley, 2001).

CHAPTER 4
Use Cases

THIS CHAPTER DESCRIBES THE PRIMARY MEANS by which you can use the UML to capture functional requirements. You express these requirements in terms of the specific actions that external entities and the system perform in executing required and optional behavior.

Actors and Use Cases

An *actor* represents one of the following things:

- A role that a user can play with regard to a system

- An entity, such as another system or a database, that resides outside the system

The UML notation for an actor is a stick figure with a short descriptive name, as shown in Figure 4-1.

Customer   Shipping System   Accountant

Figure 4-1. Actors (primary notation)

You can also show an actor using a stereotyped class or a user-defined icon (see Figure 4-2 for examples of both).

Figure 4-2. Actors (secondary notation)

> **NOTE** The name of an actor should *not* be that of a particular person; instead, it should identify a role or set of roles that a human being, an external system, or a part of the system being built will play relative to one or more use cases. Note also that a single physical entity may be modeled by several different actors and, conversely, a given actor may be played by multiple physical entities.

A *use case* is a sequence of actions performed by an actor and the system that yields an observable result, or set of results, of value for one or more actors.

The standard notation for a use case is an ellipse combined with a short name that contains an active verb and (usually) a noun phrase (see Figure 4-3).

Search by Author   Produce Shipping Manifest   Print GL Report

Figure 4-3. Use cases (primary notation)

The name of a use case can appear either within the ellipse or below it.

The text of a use case describes possible paths through the use case. Two kinds of flows of events are associated with use cases. These are as follows:

- The *main flow of events* (sometimes referred to as the *basic course of action*) is the sunny-day scenario, the main start-to-finish path that the actor and the system follow under normal circumstances. The assumption is that the primary actor doesn't make any mistakes, and the system generates no errors. A use case always has a main flow of events.

- An *exceptional flow of events* (or *alternate course of action*) is a path through a use case that represents an error condition or a path that the actor and the system take less frequently. A use case often has at least one exceptional flow of events.

Each unique execution of a use case represents a *use case instance.*

A use case can be associated with one or more *subjects.* For example, the subject may be a collaboration (see the section "Collaborations" in Chapter 1), and the use case would express the conditions that something interacting with that collaboration would need to meet in order to gain full access to the services that the collaboration offers. (Note that a subject can also be associated with more than one use case.) A subject may also "own" a use case, which is represented using the notation shown in Figure 4-4.

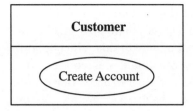

Figure 4-4. Subject owning use case

Actors and use cases appear on use case diagrams, which are described later in this chapter.

Qualities of a Good Use Case

The following guidelines have proven useful in producing tight, easy-to-understand use cases in a variety of contexts:

- **Use active voice, and speak from the actor's perspective.** For some reason, engineers and other technically inclined people tend to rely heavily on passive voice: "The connection is made," "The item is selected by the customer," and so forth. You should always express use cases in active voice. After all, you wouldn't expect to see a user manual written in passive voice, and there's a direct correlation between use cases and user manual text. (The most significant difference is that the latter is written in what's called the second-person imperative, with an unspoken "you," whereas use case text is written in the third person, in terms of specific actors and the system.)

- **Use present tense.** Requirements are usually written in the future tense: "The system shall do this and that," "The throughput of the system shall meet the following parameters." Each sentence of a use case should appear in the present tense: "The Customer selects the item," "The system makes the connection." This includes the text for alternate courses. (For example, "If the Customer selects a different item, the system comes to a grinding halt.") Keeping all the text in a consistent form makes it easier for its readers to trace the different paths through the basic course and alternate courses.

- **Express your text in the form of "call and response."** The basic form of your use case text should be "The [actor] does this" and "The system does that." The actor may do more than one thing consecutively, and the same holds true for the system, but the text should reflect the fact that the actor performs some action and the system responds accordingly. There shouldn't be any extraneous text.

- **Write your text in no more than three paragraphs.** One of the guiding principles of object-oriented design is that a class should do a small number of things well, and nothing else. Why not adhere to this principle with use cases as well? A use case should address one functional requirement, or perhaps a very small set of requirements, and do it in a way that's obvious to anyone who reads it. Anything more than a few paragraphs, and you probably have a candidate for another use case. (See the section "Organizing Use Cases," later in the chapter, for a discussion of how to break up and organize use cases.) A sentence or two, however, is a signal that you don't have enough substance in your use case. Each use case should be a small, mobile unit that lends itself to possible reuse in other contexts.

- **Name your classes.** There are two basic kinds of classes that lend themselves to inclusion in use case text: (a) those in the domain model (see the section "Domain-Level Class Diagrams" in Chapter 3) and (b) "boundary" classes, which include those windows, HTML pages, and so on that the actors use in interacting with the system. Down the line, it's going to be easier to design against text such as "The Customer changes one or more quantities on the Edit Contents of Shopping Cart page" and "The system creates an Account for the Customer" than against less-specific text (for example, "The Customer enters some values on an HTML page"). Be careful, though, to avoid including design details. You wouldn't talk about, say, the appearance of that HTML page or exactly what happens when the system creates an Account. The idea is to provide just enough detail for the designers to understand what's needed to address the basic requirements spelled out by the use cases.

- **Establish the initial context.** You have to specify where the actor is, and what he or she is looking at, at the beginning of the use case. There are two ways to do this. The first way involves specifying the context as part of the first sentence: "The Accountant enters his or her user ID and password on the System Login window," for example. The second way involves defining a precondition: "The Accountant has brought up the System Login window." Doing this also makes it easier for someone to piece together the larger picture across a set of use cases.

- **Make sure that each use case produces at least one result of value to one or more actors, even if that result is negative.** It's important to remember that a use case can't just end floating in space—something measurable has to happen. Of course, this is generally some positive result: "The actor is logged in to the system," "The system completes the actor's task by updating the database," "The system generates a report." A use case can end on an alternate course of action, though, so "The system locks the user out of the system and sends an email to the system administrator" is also a viable result, even though it's hardly a desirable one.

- **Be exhaustive in finding alternate courses of action.** A lot of the interesting behavior associated with a system can be nicely captured within alternate courses—and it's a well-established principle that it's a lot cheaper to address this kind of behavior early in a project rather than later. A highly effective, if sometimes exhausting, way to root out alternate courses is to "challenge" every sentence of the basic course. In other words, ask repeatedly, "What can the actor do differently—or wrong—at this point?" or "What can go wrong internally at this point?" Remember two things while you're doing this. First, you don't need to account for generic failure conditions—network down, database inaccessible—within each use case; focus on those things that might happen in the specific context of the use case. Second, remember to take into account not only the novice/unsophisticated user but also the malicious user, the person who tries things he or she shouldn't just to see what might happen.

There are a couple of good methods for pointing to alternate courses from within the basic course. One surefire way to signal the presence of an alternate course involves using words such as *validates*, *verifies*, and *ensures* within the basic course. Each time one of these words appears, there's at least one associated alternate course, by definition, to account for the system's inability to validate, verify, or ensure the specified condition. For example, the basic course might say, "The system verifies that the credit card number that the Customer entered matches one of the numbers it has recorded for that Customer," while the corresponding alternate course might read, "If the system cannot match the entered credit card number to any of its stored values, it displays an error message and prompts the Customer to enter a different number." Another way to indicate the presence of an alternate course involves using labels for the alternate courses and then embedding those labels in the basic course. For example, an alternate course might have a label A1, and that label would appear in parentheses after the relevant statement(s) in the basic course.

Example Use Cases

Let's look at a couple of sample use cases. We start by walking through how a use case named Log In, associated with an Internet bookstore, might have come into existence.

You first establish where the actor is, and what he or she does to initiate the use case. The steps may be as follows:

1. The Customer clicks the Login button on the Home Page.

2. The use case describes the system's response:

    `The system displays the Login Page.`

The rest of the basic course of action for this use case describes the actions that the actor performs in order to log in to the bookstore, and the actions that the system performs along the way as well:

3. The Customer enters his or her user ID and password and then clicks the OK button. The system validates the login information against the persistent Account data and then returns the Customer to the Home Page.

Remember that the Account class you defined in Chapter 1 (see Figure 1-3) contains three attributes, two of which are `ID` and `password`. As mentioned in the previous section, it's good practice to make explicit connections to domain model classes within use case text; you can certainly extend this principle to the attribute level as appropriate.

As you can see, the basic course addresses the sunny-day scenario: It assumes that nothing will go wrong. However, a good use case accounts for as many alternate paths and error conditions as possible. In this case, there are two kinds of alternate courses that we need to address. These are as follows:

-   The Customer can perform some other action before logging in. This leads to the following alternate courses:

    If the Customer clicks the New Account button, the system displays the Create New Account page.

    If the Customer enters his or her user ID and then clicks the Reminder Word button, the system displays a dialog box containing the reminder word stored for that Customer. When the Customer clicks the OK button, the system returns the Customer to the Home Page.

-   The system is unable to validate a value that the Customer provided and thus is unable to complete the login process. The following courses of action are possible:

If the Customer enters a user ID that the system does not recognize, the system displays the Create New Account page.

If the Customer enters an incorrect password, the system prompts the Customer to reenter his or her password.

If the Customer enters an incorrect password three times, the system displays a page telling the Customer that he or she should contact customer service.

Note how the reader of a use case can see where each alternate course branches out from the basic course.

Another key principle is that a use case has to end with the system providing some result of value to an actor. The basic course of Log In reflects that the Customer is logged in to the system at the end of the use case. The alternate courses also reflect that result, albeit in somewhat different ways. In two cases, the Customer ends up back at the Home Page, and the assumption is that he or she will proceed with the basic course of action. In another case, the system takes the Customer to a different page; this may not be a desirable option from his or her standpoint, but it's still a result of value. And in two cases, the system displays a new page that the Customer can use to create a new account. (Let's assume that some use case diagram for our bookstore will show that Log In has a connection with a Create New Account use case.)

Our second, more complicated use case is called Write Customer Review. It illustrates more basic principles discussed previously: active voice from the actor's perspective, present tense, a result of value, no more than three paragraphs, and alternate courses of action that reflect different paths.

Basic Course

The Customer clicks the Review This Book button on the Book Page. The system displays a page entitled Write a Review.

The Customer selects a rating for the given Book, types a title for his or her review, and then types the review itself. Then the Customer indicates whether the system should display his or her name or email address, or both, in connection with the review.

When the Customer has finished selecting and entering information, he or she clicks the Preview My Review button. The system displays a Look Over Your Review page that contains the information that the Customer provided. The Customer clicks the Save button. The system stores the information associated with the Review and returns the Customer to the Book Page.

Alternate Courses

If the Customer clicks the Review Guidelines button on the Book Page, the system displays the Customer Review Guidelines page. When the Customer clicks the OK button on that page, the system returns the Customer to the Book Page.

If the Customer clicks the Edit button on the Look Over My Review page, the system allows the Customer to make changes to any of the information that he or she provided on the Write a Review page. When the Customer clicks the Save button, the system stores the review information and returns the Customer to the Book Page.

Organizing Use Cases

The UML offers three constructs for factoring out common behavior and variant paths for use cases. The following subsections describe these constructs.

Include

Within an *include* relationship, one use case *explicitly* includes the behavior of another use case at a specified point within a course of action.

The included use case doesn't stand alone; it has to be connected with one or more base use cases. The include mechanism is very useful for factoring out behavior that would otherwise appear within multiple use cases.

Within Figure 4-5, the Add to Wish List and Check Out use cases include the behavior captured within the Log In use case, because a Customer must be logged in before he or she can add a book to a wish list or make a purchase.

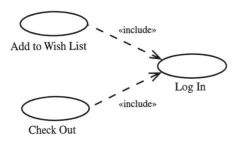

Figure 4-5. Include

Extend

Within an *extend* relationship, a base use case *implicitly* includes the behavior of another use case at one or more specified points. These points are called *extension points*.

You generally use this construct to factor out behavior that's optional or that occurs only under certain conditions. One way to use extends is in creating a new use case in response to an alternate course of action having several steps associated with it.

Figure 4-6 shows that a Customer has the option of canceling an Order in conjunction with checking the status of that Order.

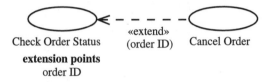

Figure 4-6. Extend

If it's desirable to show an explanation of when a use case extension comes into play, you can show this in a note, as illustrated in Figure 4-7.

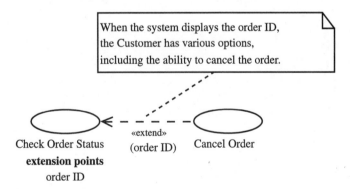

Figure 4-7. Explaining a use case extension

NOTE You have the option of using standard class notation to represent a use case, with the use case ellipse in the name compartment, and to add one or more compartments to the class box to hold relevant information—for example, multiple extension points. See Figure 4-8.

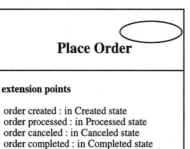

Figure 4-8. Use cases (secondary notation)

Use Case Generalization

Generalization works the same way for use cases as it does for classes (see the section "Generalization" in Chapter 2): A parent use case defines behavior that its children can inherit, and the children can add to or override that behavior.

Figure 4-9 shows use cases that describe three different searches that a Customer can perform, all of which use the basic search technique defined by the Perform Search use case.

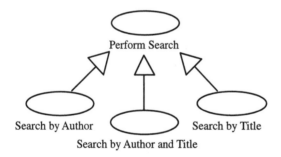

Figure 4-9. Use case generalization

> **NOTE** You can also use generalization with actors. For example, there might be a general Accounting Personnel actor, which has certain privileges, and then Accountant and Accounting Clerk actors that represent more specialized usage privileges than those actors have.

Use Case Diagrams

A *use case diagram* shows a set of use cases and actors and the relationships among them. Figure 4-10 shows an example of a use case diagram.

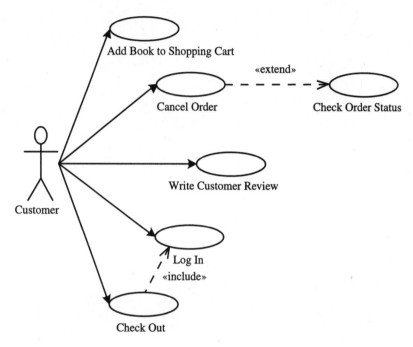

Figure 4-10. Use case diagram

It's a good idea to draw one use case diagram per actor. You can also use different layers of use case diagrams to good effect. For example, you might have an "executive summary" layer that shows only the use cases of most general interest, and then subsequent layers would show more specialized use cases.

Looking Ahead

In the next chapter, you take a look at a UML construct that you can use to help you organize conceptually related elements of your models.

CHAPTER 5

Packages

THIS CHAPTER DESCRIBES THE MEANS by which you can use the UML to group various model elements that are conceptually related.

Package Fundamentals

A *package* is a grouping of pieces of a model. Packages are very useful in managing models. They're also quite helpful in grouping related items, such as use cases, in order to make it easier to break up work among subteams.

A package can contain one or more kinds of model elements, each of which must have a unique name within the package. In a package, there can just be classes (see Chapter 1), classes and class diagrams (see Chapter 3), just use cases (see Chapter 4), or a number of different kinds of constructs and diagrams. The only rule is that each element of a model can belong directly to only one package. (In UML terms, a model is basically a package that contains other packages.) Note, though, that a package is a *conceptual* grouping; the system will probably not be built along package boundaries.

A UML package appears as a tabbed folder. There are the following three variations:

- The package name appears in the body of the folder, and the contents are hidden from view (see Figure 5-1).

Figure 5-1. Package (no members shown)

- The name of the package appears within the tab, and the contents of the package are listed in the body of the folder (see Figure 5-2).

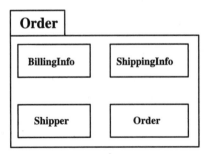

Figure 5-2. Package (members shown internally)

- The package name appears in the body of the folder, and the contents are shown outside the folder (see Figure 5-3).

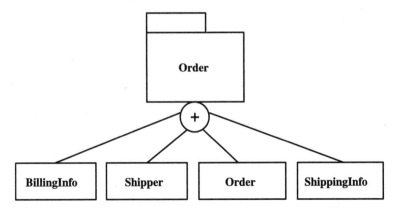

Figure 5-3. Package (members shown externally)

A package name should be short and simple; it should convey the essence of the contents of the package.

You can also show the visibility of the elements within a package. The available options are public (+), which means that any other element can "see" the given element, and private (–), which means that only other elements within the same package can see the given element.

Import and Access

A package can add external model elements by reference. If the visibility of a given element is public, the package performs an *import*; if the visibility is private, the package performs an *access*. Both import and access are shown as stereotyped dependencies, with the dependent package receiving the import or access. Figure 5-4 shows examples of both.

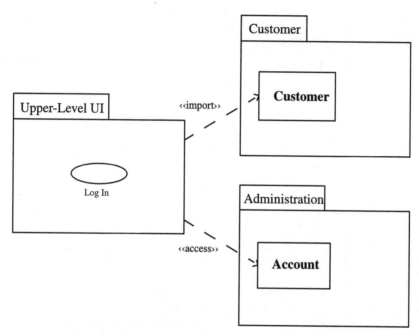

Figure 5-4. Element import and access

Note that if a package imports an element with the same name as an element contained within the package, the import must have an associated alias. Figure 5-5 shows an example of an import with an alias.

The WebServer package refers to the Book class within the Catalog package as CatalogBook going forward. (To avoid confusion, it's probably a good idea to rename one or the other Book class rather than relying on an alias.)

Import and access work the same ways on the package level. Figure 5-6 shows an example of a package import.

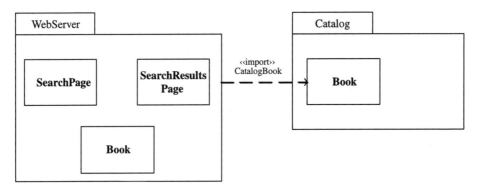

Figure 5-5. Element import with alias

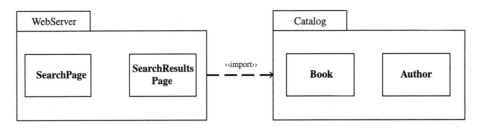

Figure 5-6. Package import

As a result of this import, the WebServer package can treat the Book and Author classes as if they belonged to it and not to the Catalog package.

A special case of a package import involves the «modelLibrary» stereotype. This stereotype signifies that the client package is using the source package as a library of shared model elements. For example, you might have a package of datatypes (see the section "Other Stereotypes on Classes" in Chapter 1) that you want to share among various packages.

Merging Packages

The package merge feature of the UML allows you to merge the contents of a target package into a source package. This is useful when elements of the same name are intended to represent the same basic concepts.

The resulting merged package combines elements using generalization (see the section "Generalization" in Chapter 2) and redefinitions. The following basic rules apply:

- All existing relationships are retained intact.

- Each element within one of the packages participating in the merger gets subclassed under the original element of the same name, with the latter named *package name:element name*. This is necessary because the super-class elements may have brought additional properties that need to be propagated to the subclass elements.

Figure 5-7 shows an example of a package merge.

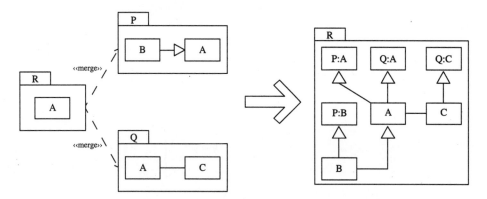

Figure 5-7. Package merge

Package Diagrams

A *package diagram* shows the contents of a package, which can include nested packages and, optionally, the relationships among those contents. Figure 5-8 shows an example of a package diagram.

You see other examples of package diagrams throughout the book.

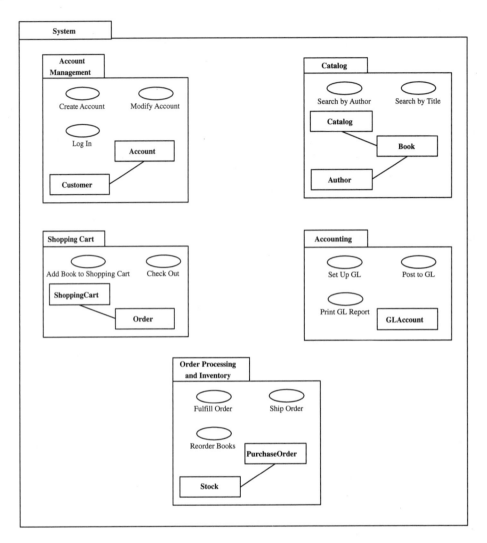

Figure 5-8. Package diagram

Looking Ahead

In the next chapter, you get back to exploring how to do dynamic modeling within the UML, this time at a fairly detailed level.

CHAPTER 6

Events, Actions, and Activities

WE'VE BEEN MOSTLY EXPLORING THE STATIC SIDE of UML modeling, with the exception of use cases, which model behavior on a fairly abstract level. Now it's time to dig deeper into the dynamic side of the UML.

This chapter explores the following three areas:

- The various ways by which object behavior is initiated

- The UML's *action model,* which defines the individual, primitive functions that serve as the lowest (in other words, least abstract) level of behavior specification

- Activities, which provide control and data sequencing constraints among actions—as well as inputs and outputs for those actions—and nested structuring mechanisms for control and scope

Signals, Triggers, and Events

A *signal* is a notification of some kind that an object dispatches asynchronously to one or more other objects. The attributes of a signal serve as its parameters.

Figure 6-1 indicates the following ways to show a signal using UML:

- As a standard stereotype label attached to a class

- As part of a list within an extra compartment attached to the bottom of a class box

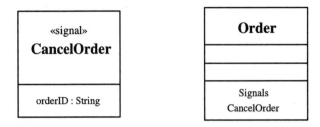

Figure 6-1. Signals

A *reception* is a declaration that a particular class or interface (see the section "Interfaces, Ports, and Connectors" in Chapter 1) is prepared to react to the receipt of a given signal. Figure 6-2 shows the notation for a reception.

Figure 6-2. Reception

You indicate the transmission of a signal with the «send» stereotype attached to a dependency arrow. (The send dependency is a type of usage dependency; see the section "Dependencies" in Chapter 2.) Within Figure 6-3, the login operation sends a signal to the SecurityManager object once the current user has tried unsuccessfully three times to log in to the system.

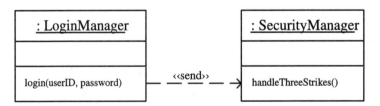

Figure 6-3. Send dependency

When the SecurityManager object is ready to deal with the signal, the object invokes its handleThreeStrikes method on itself.

A *trigger* represents an occurrence of an *event,* which is something of significance to one or more objects that may cause the execution of some behavior associated with the object(s).

The UML defines the following four kinds of triggers:

- A *call trigger* represents the reception of a request to call a specific operation belonging to a given class (which becomes a call on a method on an object that represents an instance of that class).

- A *change trigger* represents an event that occurs when a Boolean expression becomes True as a result of a change in value of one or more attributes or associations. You express a change event using the word *when* (for example, when midnight or when maximumLoops =100).

- A *signal trigger* represents the reception of a particular signal.

- A *time trigger* represents an event that occurs after a specified period of time. You express a time event using the word *after* followed by an expression of absolute or relative time (for example, after 5 seconds or after [15 minutes since last keyboard or mouse action]).

Actions

An *action* is an executable primitive assignment or computation that receives a set of input values and produces a change of state and/or the return of output values. (A change of state of an object is reflected by changes to the values of one or more of its attributes.)

The notation for an action is a rectangle with rounded corners. Figure 6-4 shows three examples of actions.

Look up country code

Compute shipping cost

Set fulfillment flag

Figure 6-4. Actions

Unless noted otherwise, all actions use this basic notation.

Just as you can specify constraints on operations (see the section "More About Operations" in Chapter 1), you can specify them on actions.

A *local precondition* is a condition that must hold true when execution of an action begins. Figure 6-5 shows an example of a local precondition.

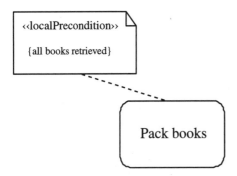

Figure 6-5. Local precondition

A *local postcondition* is a condition that must hold true when execution of an action ends. Figure 6-6 shows an example of a local postcondition.

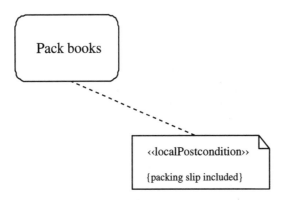

Figure 6-6. Local postcondition

NOTE   See the section "More About Operations" in Chapter 1 to learn more about the Object Constraint Language (OCL), which you can use to specify local preconditions and local postconditions.

A *pin* is a modeling element for an input to or output from an action. The input values to an action come from an *input pin;* the output values from an action go to an *output pin.*

A pin appears as a small rectangle on one side of the action symbol, as shown in Figure 6-7.

Figure 6-7. Pins

Generally, input pins appear on the left side of the action symbol, while output pins appear on the right side, but this convention isn't required.

The UML defines two categories of actions: intermediate actions and complete actions.

Intermediate Actions

Intermediate actions are action primitives that either carry out a computation or access object memory, but never both.

The following subsections describe the various kinds of intermediate actions.

Invocation Actions

There are five kinds of actions that involve invoking object behavior. These actions are described as follows:

- A *broadcast signal action* transmits an instance of a specified signal to a set of potential target objects in the system. The signal's arguments, which in turn become available to each object that receives the signal, are specified on a particular input pin. (The UML doesn't offer any guidance as to how to specify the set of target objects.) This kind of action doesn't receive any response from the invoked behavior.

- A *call behavior action* invokes a specified behavior directly, either synchronously or asynchronously. The action receives arguments from particular input pins; the behavior places its result(s) on a particular output pin.

The symbol for a regular call behavior action is the same as that for a generic action. However, if the invocation involves starting an activity, the name of the activity appears within the action symbol along with a rake symbol, as shown in Figure 6-8.

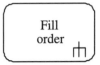

Figure 6-8. Call behavior action invoking activity

- A *call operation action* sends a message to a specified object to call a specified method, either synchronously or asynchronously. The method places its result(s) on a particular output pin.

- A *send object action* transmits a specified object to a specified target object as a signal.

- A *send signal action* creates an instance of a specified signal and transmits it to a specified target object. Figure 6-9 shows an example of a send signal action.

Figure 6-9. Send signal action

Intermediate Read and Write Actions

Read and write actions read values from and write values to objects, attributes, link objects, and variables; these actions also create and destroy these things.

There are four kinds of read and write actions that involve objects. They are described as follows:

- A *create object action* creates an object belonging to a specified classifier and then places that object on a particular output pin.

- A *destroy object action* destroys an object specified on a particular input pin.

- A *read self action* retrieves the object to which the enclosing activity belongs and then places the object on a particular output pin.

- A *test identity action* determines whether two values, specified on separate input pins, refer to the same specified object and then places True if they do, or False if they don't, on a particular output pin.

The following six kinds of read and write actions involve structural features of classifiers. (These structural features generally take the form of attributes.)

- An *add structural feature value action* adds one or more values, specified on a particular input pin, to a specified structural feature.

- A *clear structural feature action* deletes all values from a specified structural feature.

- A *duration observation action* measures a duration during system execution. (A *duration* represents the length of time between the occurrence of two particular events.)

- A *read structural feature action* retrieves the values of a specified structural feature and then puts these values on a particular output pin.

- A *remove structural feature value action* deletes a value, specified on a particular input pin, from a specified structural feature.

- A *time observation action* measures the current time, according to the system clock, during system execution.

There are four kinds of actions that involve links (instances of associations). These actions are described as follows:

- A *clear association action* destroys all links that are instances of a particular association connected to an object specified on a particular input pin.

- A *create link action* creates a link using the association ends specified by two or more *link end creation data* entities.

- A *destroy link action* destroys the link(s) or link object(s) specified by two or more *link end data* entities.

- A *read link action* navigates across a link, specified by two link end data entities, to retrieve the object(s) at one end and then places the object(s) on a particular output pin.

The following four kinds of actions involve *variables,* which in this context are elements for passing data between actions indirectly:

- An *add variable value action* adds one or more values, specified on a particular input pin, to a given variable.

- A *clear variable action* deletes all values from a given variable.

- A *read variable action* reads the values of a given variable and puts them on a specified output pin.

- A *remove variable value action* deletes a value, specified on a particular input pin, from a given variable.

Apply Function Action

An *apply function action* applies a specified primitive function to a set of values that the action retrieves from a specified input pin and then places the return values on a specified output pin. (A *primitive function* is a predefined mathematical function, specified in an external language, that depends only on input values, as opposed to values from memory or objects. Examples of primitive functions include those that compute square roots and logarithms.)

Complete Actions

Complete actions aggregate intermediate actions. The following subsections describe the various kinds of complete actions.

Accept and Reply Actions

The following four kinds of actions involve responding to operation calls and the occurrences of events:

- An *accept call action* represents the receipt of a synchronous call request for an operation specified by a particular call trigger (see the section "Signals, Triggers, and Events," earlier in this chapter). The action produces a token for the specified output pin that contains information that is eventually sent back to the caller by a reply action (defined later in this list).

- An *accept signal action* waits for the occurrence of a signal of the type, or any subtype of that type, specified by a particular trigger. When this event occurs, the action places the signal object on the specified output pin. Figure 6-10 shows an example of an accept signal action and the behavior it invokes.

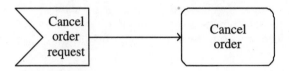

Figure 6-10. Accept signal action

- An *accept time event action* waits for an occurrence of a time event that meets the criteria specified by a particular trigger. When this event occurs, the action places the time at which the event occurred on the specified output pin. Figure 6-11 shows an example of an accept time event action and the behavior it invokes.

Figure 6-11. Accept time event action

- A *reply action* accepts a set of return values and a token that contains return information, produced by a previous accept call action (defined earlier in this list), from the specified input pin. The relevant call trigger then retrieves these values and the token, which completes the call.

Complete Object Actions

The following four kinds of actions involve performing functions with objects and the classifiers to which they belong:

- A *read extent action* retrieves all runtime instances of a specified class that are currently in existence, and then places this "extent" on a particular output pin.

- A *read is classified object action* determines whether an object, specified on a particular input pin, belongs to a particular class and then places True if it does, or False if it doesn't, on a particular output pin.

NOTE   You can specify whether the class must be the "direct" class. The default is that the class must be direct—in other words, directly above the given class in the class hierarchy—for the action to return True.

- A *reclassify object action* changes the class(es), from a specified "old" set to a specified "new" set, to which an object, specified on a particular input pin, belongs.

- A *start owned behavior action* starts the behavior owned by the object specified on a particular input pin.

Complete Read and Write Actions

Three kinds of actions involve reading from and creating *link objects*, which are instances of association classes (see the section "Association Classes" in Chapter 2). These actions are described as follows:

- A *create link object action* creates a link object, using the association ends, and perhaps the qualifier values, specified by two or more specified link end creation data entities (see the section "Intermediate Read and Write Actions," earlier in this chapter), and then places the link object on the specified output pin. (A *qualifier* is an attribute that defines a partition of a set of instances with respect to the object at the other end of a link.)

- A *read link object end action* reads the link object, specified on a particular input pin, at a specified end, and then places the object on the specified output pin.

- A *read link object end qualifier action* reads the value of a specified qualifier, connected with a link object specified on a particular input pin, and then places the qualifier value on the specified output pin.

Raise Exception Action

A *raise exception action* turns the value on the specified input pin into an *exception,* which is a special kind of signal that a class can throw or receive in response to a failure during system execution.

There are two good ways to model an exception, as follows:

- Create a standard class box that uses stereotype notation.

- Create a class box that has an extra compartment at the bottom that contains a list of exceptions to which the class can respond.

Figure 6-12 shows an example using both notations.

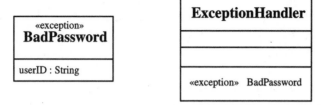

Figure 6-12. Exceptions

Exceptions should eventually be handled by an exception handler. (Exception handlers are discussed later in this chapter.)

Activities, Activity Nodes, and Activity Edges

The following subsections describe various aspects of activities, which reside at the next level of abstraction up from actions.

Activities

An *activity* is an ongoing nonatomic (in other words, interruptible) execution of a series of actions (see the section "Actions," earlier in this chapter).

A simple activity appears in the same shape as an action (see the section "Actions," earlier in this chapter). For a complex activity, you can show *activity nodes,* which are placeholders for one or more steps within an activity, and *activity edges,* which are connections between activity nodes. (Actions are kinds of activity nodes.) *Tokens* control the flow of data and/or control within an activity; a token can contain an object, a piece of data, or a locus of control.

Figure 6-13 shows the notation for a complex activity, which includes nodes and edges plus a border and a name for the activity, displayed in the upper-left corner.

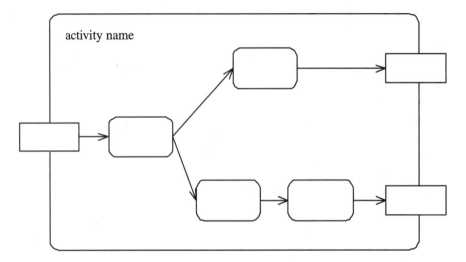

Figure 6-13. Complex activity

The rectangles on the edges of the diagram represent *activity parameter nodes,* which are special types of activity nodes that appear at the beginning or end of flows to accept inputs to an activity from another activity or to provide outputs from the activity to another activity.

Activity Nodes

The following subsections describe the various kinds of activity nodes.

Control Nodes

Control nodes coordinate flows among other activity nodes. There are seven kinds of control nodes; they are described as follows:

- An *initial node* is where the flow of control starts when an activity is invoked. Figure 6-14 shows the notation for an initial node.

Figure 6-14. Initial node

- A *final node* is a control node at which one or more flows within the given activity stop. There are two types of final nodes: flow final nodes and activity final nodes.

  A *flow final node* terminates a particular flow. Figure 6-15 shows the notation for a flow final node.

Figure 6-15. Flow final node

  An *activity final node* terminates all flows within the activity and thus terminates the activity itself. Figure 6-16 shows the notation for an activity final node.

Figure 6-16. Activity final node

- A *decision node* offers a choice among two or more outgoing activity edges, each of which has a guard, which is a Boolean expression that must resolve to True before the associated path can be taken.

  A decision node appears as a diamond, as shown in Figure 6-17.

  You can apply the «decisionInput» stereotype to a decision node to specify a decision criterion instead of spelling out the possible values on the activity edges. Figure 6-18 shows an example of this stereotype.

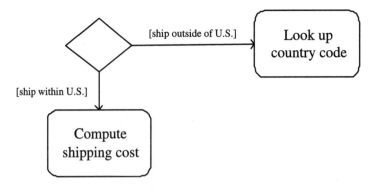

Figure 6-17. Decision node

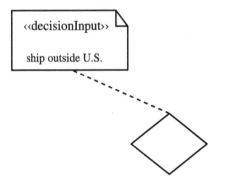

Figure 6-18. Decision input

- A *merge node* brings together multiple alternate control flows. Figure 6-19 shows the notation for a merge node, which is the same as that for a decision node.

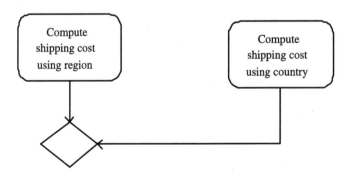

Figure 6-19. Merge node

- A *fork node* splits a flow into multiple concurrent flows. Figure 6-20 shows the notation for a fork node, which is a long, thin black rectangle.

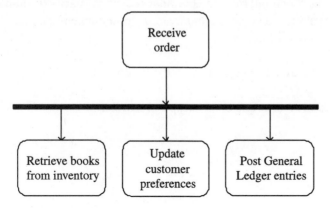

Figure 6-20. Fork node

- A *join node* synchronizes multiple control flows. Figure 6-21 shows the notation for a join node, which is the same as that for a fork node.

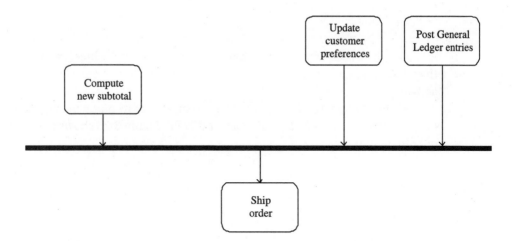

Figure 6-21. Join node

Executable Node

An *executable node* is an activity node that may be executed.

An executable node owns one or more *exception handlers*. Each handler specifies an executable node to execute in case a specified exception occurs during the execution of another executable node.

An exception handler appears as the combination of the following two items:

- A "lightning bolt" symbol from the boundary of the primary executable node to a small square on the boundary of the executable node that processes the exception

- The name of the exception type next to the lightning bolt

Figure 6-22 shows an example of an exception handler.

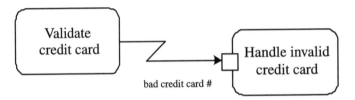

Figure 6-22. Exception handler

Object Nodes

An *object node* is an activity node that provides and accepts objects and data as they flow into and out of invoked behaviors in the context of the execution of an activity.

An object node usually appears as a rectangle with its name inside. If the node represents a signal, the notation is different. Figure 6-23 shows examples of both notations.

Figure 6-23. Object nodes

There are four kinds of object nodes, each of which may have a specialized notation. These object nodes are described as follows:

- An *activity parameter node* is a special type of activity node (described in the section "Activities," earlier in this chapter).

- A *central buffer node* accepts tokens from an "upstream" object node and passes them along to a "downstream" object node.

  A *data store node* is a special type of central buffer node that handles persistent information. Figure 6-24 shows an example of a data store node.

Figure 6-24. Data store node

- An *expansion node* is an object node that indicates a flow across the boundary of an expansion region. (Expansion regions are discussed in the section "Structured Activity Nodes," later in this chapter.) A flow into a region contains a collection that is broken into its individual elements inside the region; the region then executes once per element. A flow out of a region combines individual elements into a collection for use outside the region.

- A *pin* is a type of object node (discussed in the section "Actions," earlier in this chapter).

Activity Edges

An activity edge may have a guard on it. It may also have a name.

Figure 6-25 shows an example of an activity edge that connects two activity nodes.

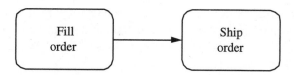

Figure 6-25. Activity edge

You can also use connector symbols for graphical convenience, as shown in Figure 6-26.

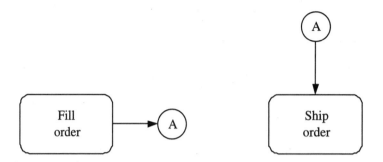

Figure 6-26. Activity edge with connectors

There are two kinds of activity edges, as follows:

- A *control flow* only passes control tokens.

- An *object flow* can have objects or data passing along it.

Activity Groups

An *activity group* is a grouping of activity nodes and activity edges. The following subsections describe the various kinds of activity groups.

Activity Partitions

An *activity partition* identifies actions that have some characteristics in common. This partition divides activity nodes and activity edges to constrain, and show a view of, the contained nodes, but it doesn't affect the flows within the given activity.

Activity partitions are represented by *swimlanes,* which are pairs of parallel vertical or horizontal lines on an activity diagram (discussed later in the chapter). Figure 6-27 shows an excerpt of an activity diagram with swimlanes.

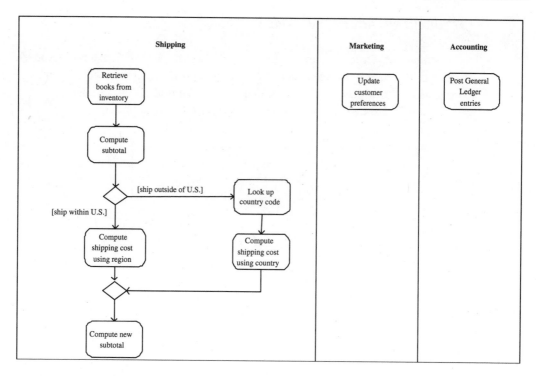

Figure 6-27. Swimlanes

Interruptible Activity Regions

An *interruptible activity region* supports interrupts by terminating any tokens and behaviors connected with the activity nodes within the region when an interrupt arrives.

An interruptible activity region appears as a dashed, round-cornered rectangle drawn around the nodes it contains. An interrupting activity edge appears as a "lightning bolt" coming from a node within the rectangle. Figure 6-28 shows the notation of an interruptible activity region.

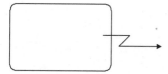

Figure 6-28. Interruptible activity region

Structured Activity Nodes

A *structured activity node* is an executable node (see the section "Executable Node," earlier in the chapter) that represents a structured portion of a given activity that isn't shared with any other structured node, except for nodes that are nested.

Figure 6-29 shows the notation for a structured activity node.

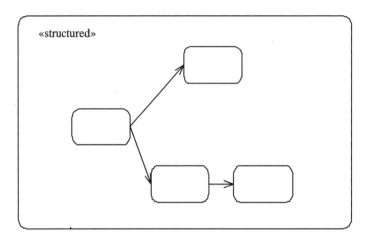

Figure 6-29. Structured activity node

There are three kinds of structured activity nodes, which are described as follows:

- A *conditional node* represents an exclusive choice among some number of alternatives. Each alternative is expressed in the form of a *clause,* which is a combination of a test and a body section such that if execution of the test results in the value True, the body section is executed.

- An *expansion region* executes once for each element within a given collection of values in a particular expansion node (see the section "Object Nodes," earlier in this chapter). These executions occur based on a specified expansion kind; the possible values are iterative (the executions are dependent and thus must be executed one at a time), parallel (the executions are independent and thus may be executed concurrently), and stream (a stream of collection elements flows into a single execution). The results of the executions may form one or more new expansion nodes.

  An expansion region is shown as a dashed box with rounded corners, with the expansion kind value in the upper-left corner and input and output expansion nodes appearing as small rectangles divided by vertical bars into small compartments on the boundaries of the box. Figure 6-30 shows an example of an expansion region.

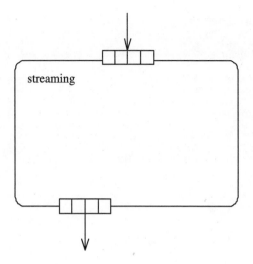

Figure 6-30. Expansion region

Figure 6-31 shows a shorthand notation that you can use if the expansion region has only one activity node.

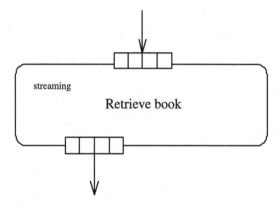

Figure 6-31. Expansion region with one node

- A *loop node* represents a loop with setup, test, and body sections. The setup section is executed once on entry to the loop; the test and body sections are executed repeatedly until the test produces False.

Activity Diagrams

An *activity diagram* illustrates the flow(s) of control among activities and actions associated with a particular object or set of objects.

Modelers typically use activity diagrams to illustrate the following:

- The flow of a complicated use case

- A workflow across use cases

- The logic of an algorithm

Figure 6-32 shows an excerpt from an example activity diagram.

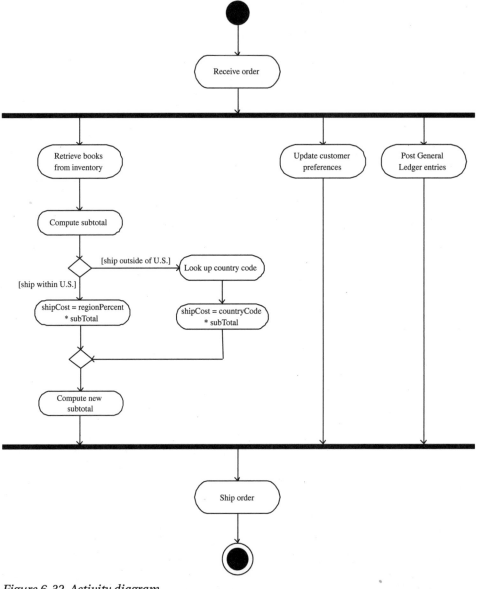

Figure 6-32. Activity diagram

Since activity diagrams tend to contain design-level details, it makes sense to put them into design-level packages, such as the one shown in Figure 6-33.

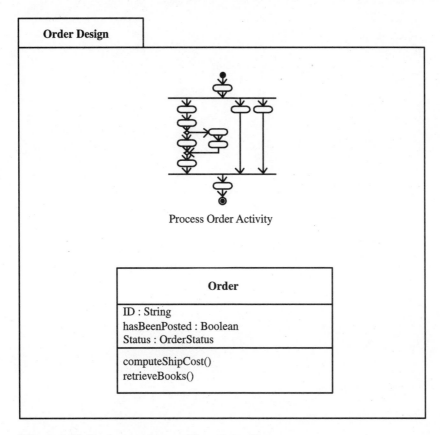

Figure 6-33. Design package with activity diagram

Looking Ahead

The next chapter discusses constructs that you can use to go inside of individual objects and model their behavior in terms of the states in which an object can reside and the transitions that can happen between those states.

CHAPTER 7

State Machines

THIS CHAPTER ADDRESSES THE **UML** CONSTRUCTS that you can use to model discrete object behavior in terms of the states an object can reside in and the transitions that can happen between those states. The chapter addresses both *behavioral state machines,* which specify sequences of states that objects go through during their lifetimes in response to events and the responses that the objects make to those events, and *protocol state machines,* which specify which operations of a given class can be called when instances of that class are in particular states and under which conditions.

States and Transitions

A *state* is a condition in which an object can be at some point during its lifetime, for some finite amount of time.

An object can do any or all of the following while it's in a particular state:

- Perform an activity (see the section "Activities, Activity Nodes, and Activity Edges" in Chapter 6)

- Wait for an event (see the section "Signals, Triggers, and Events" in Chapter 6 for a list of events that the UML supports)

- Satisfy one or more conditions

The UML notation for a state is a rectangle with rounded corners. Figure 7-1 shows three sample states in which an Order object can reside.

Figure 7-1. States

When an Order is in the Posting state, it performs an activity that involves other objects—in this case, objects that belong to the Accounting portion of the system. (It's fairly common for other objects to be involved with a given object's activities.) The Retrieving Books state involves an ongoing activity but no outside objects. The Shipped state is an example of a state in which an object has satisfied some condition.

A *transition* is a change of an object from one state (the *source state*) to another (the *target state*).

A transition "fires" when an event of interest to the given object occurs. (The event "triggers" the transition.) Alternatively, a transition may fire unconditionally when the object is ready to move from one state to another, generally because the activity associated with the source state is complete. This is called a *triggerless transition*.

There may also be an action associated with a triggered transition. Unless there's also a guard (discussed later in this section), this action executes unconditionally before the object enters the target state.

An object doesn't have to go from one state to a different state within a transition. A *self-transition* is a transition whose source state and target state are the same.

Figure 7-2 shows some transitions that an Order object might go through.

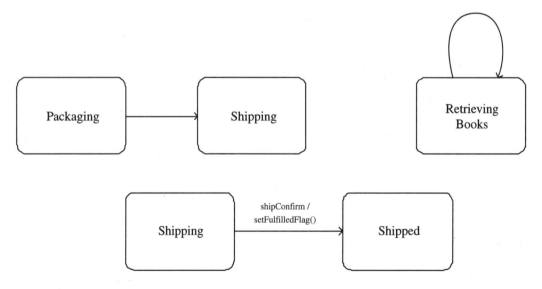

Figure 7-2. Transitions

The transition from Packaging to Shipping is triggerless, just like the ones that appear on activity diagrams (see the section "Activity Diagrams" in Chapter 6). The transition from Shipping to Shipped occurs when the shipConfirm event occurs; the Order object records the change in state by performing a call action (invoking the setFulfilledFlag method on itself). The Retrieving Books state has a self-transition.

A *guard* is a Boolean expression that must evaluate to True before a given transition can fire.

You show a guard in square brackets near the transition arrow. Various guard forms are as follows:

- If a guard is associated with an event, you use the form *eventName [guard]*. If the Boolean evaluates to False, the object ignores the event and doesn't change states.

- If you have an event, a guard, and an action, the form is *eventName [guard] / action*. Again, if the Boolean is False, the object doesn't execute the action, and no state change occurs.

- You can also have a guard by itself on a transition, which takes the form *[guard]*.

Figure 7-3 shows some guards that might apply to transitions associated with an Order object.

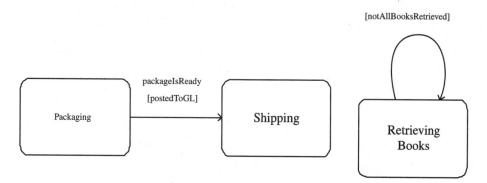

Figure 7-3. Guards

The transition between Packaging and Shipping occurs when the packageIsReady event comes in *and* it's been established that the associated Order has been posted to the General Ledger (GL). The Order object stays in the Retrieving Books state until the Order realizes that it's accumulated all the books that the Customer requested.

The symbol for a state may contain any of several other pieces of information, as follows:

- An *entry action* is an action that the object always performs immediately upon entering the given state. This appears as entry/*actionName* within the state symbol. If a self-transition occurs, the object performs the entry action. Figure 7-4 shows an example of an entry action.

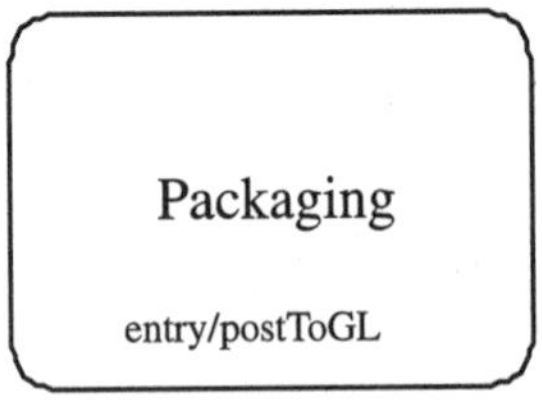

Figure 7-4. Entry action

- An *exit action*, similarly, is an action that the object always performs immediately before leaving the given state, in response to a regular transition or a self-transition. This appears in the form exit/*actionName*. Figure 7-5 shows an example of an exit action.

Figure 7-5. Exit action

In many cases, an object doesn't do anything except wait while it's in a particular state. However, you can show, within the state symbol, an activity that the object performs while it's in the state, using the notation do/*activityName*.

NOTE An activity is interruptible, which means that when an event comes in, the object is likely to stop performing the activity and respond to the event.

- An object may handle the reception of an event by performing some action while still remaining in the existing state. This is called an *internal transition*; it's shown as *eventName/actionName*. If an object makes an internal transition, it does *not* execute the exit action or the entry action. (Note how this is different from a self-transition, which *does* result in the execution of the exit action and then the entry action.)

- A *deferred event* is an event that's of interest to the object, but which the object defers handling until the object reaches a different state. This is shown as *eventName*/defer. Deferred events get put into a queue; when the object changes state, the object first checks to see whether there are events in the queue to which it can now respond. Figure 7-6 shows an example of an exit action involving a GeneralLedger object.

Figure 7-6. Deferred event

If the GeneralLedger object receives a generateReport event, the object defers responding to the event because it's in the middle of posting journal entries. When this processing is complete, and the object enters the Idle state, the object responds appropriately to the event.

Pseudostates

A *pseudostate* takes the basic form of a state, but it doesn't behave like a full state.

There are 11 kinds of pseudostates, described as follows:

- An *entry point* represents a point of entry into a state machine. Figure 7-7 shows two equivalent notations for an entry point.

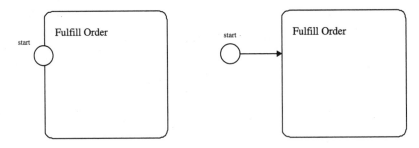

Figure 7-7. Entry point

- An *exit point* represent a point of exit from a state machine. Figure 7-8 shows two equivalent notations for an exit point.

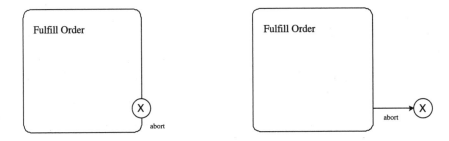

Figure 7-8. Exit point

- An *initial state* indicates the default starting place for a transition whose target is the boundary of a state. Figure 7-9 shows the notation for an initial state.

Figure 7-9. Initial state

- A *final state* indicates that the execution of part or all of an enclosing composite state (see the next section), or of an entire state machine, is complete. Figure 7-10 shows the notation for a final state.

Figure 7-10. Final state

- A *choice* makes it possible to perform a branch within which the choice of which outgoing path to take can depend on the results of actions executed before the branch occurs as well as the guards connected with the branch. Figure 7-11 shows two equivalent notations for a choice.

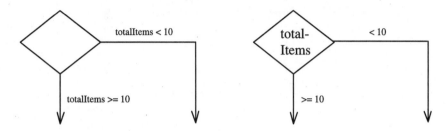

Figure 7-11. Choice

- A *fork* splits a transition into two or more transitions. Figure 7-12 shows the notation for a fork that operates on the transition coming out of the Packing Order state.

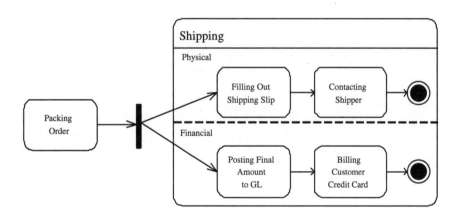

Figure 7-12. Fork

When the Order object leaves the Packing Order state, the object simultaneously enters the Filling Out Shipping Slip state and the Posting Final Amount to GL state. (The Shipping state is called a composite state; this term is discussed in the next section.)

- A *join,* conversely, merges two or more transitions. Figure 7-13 shows a join that occurs right before the transition to the Shipping Order state.

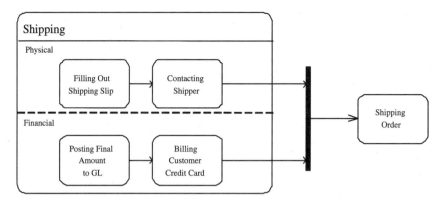

Figure 7-13. Join

When the Order object has left both the Contacting Shipper state and the Billing Customer Credit Card state, it enters the Shipping Order state.

- A *junction* makes it possible to build a single overall transition from a series of transition fragments. Within Figure 7-14, the black dot in the middle of the figure is the junction.

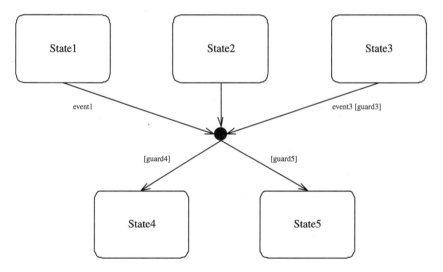

Figure 7-14. Junction

- A *shallow history* "remembers" only the outermost nested state that the given object was in before it left the enclosing composite state. You can use shallow history, then, to allow an event to interrupt an activity and then let the object pick up where it left off once it's handled that event.

The notation for shallow history is H inside a small circle. Figure 7-15 shows an example of a shallow history.

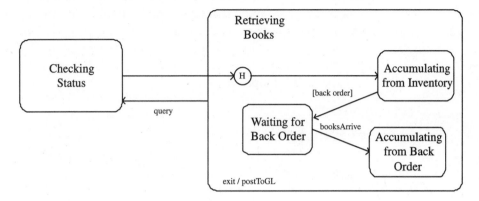

Figure 7-15. Shallow history

When a query event comes in while an Order object is in the Retrieving Books state, the system puts the current activity—in other words, whatever's going on in the current state—on hold and puts the object into the Checking Status state. When the activities associated with that state are finished, the system puts the Order back into the Retrieving Books state and the substate in which the Order resided when activity was interrupted, and the Order resumes performing the interrupted activity. (The Retrieving Books state is another example of a composite state. Composite states are discussed in the next section.)

- A *deep history* "remembers" the innermost nested state at any depth within a composite state.

  The symbol for a history state is H* inside a small circle. You could substitute this symbol for the shallow history symbol within to show, for instance, that execution should resume with the object in the Waiting for Back Order substate.

- A *terminate* represents the termination of the execution of a state machine. Figure 7-16 shows the notation for a terminate pseudostate.

Figure 7-16. Terminate pseudostate

Composite States and Submachines

The text in the section "States and Transitions" addressed what are officially called *simple states*. These are states that have no *substates* nested within them.

A state that has one or more nested substates is called a *composite state*. Composite states come in two forms: those that contain sequential, or disjoint, substates and those that contain concurrent substates. The following subsections discuss both types of composite states.

Sequential Substates

A *sequential substate* is a substate in which an object can reside to the exclusion of all other substates at that same level within the given composite state. Given two or more sequential substates at the same level, an object can be in only one of them.

Figure 7-17 shows three examples of sequential substates within the Retrieving Books composite state.

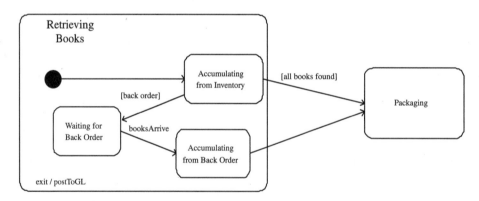

Figure 7-17. Sequential substates

When an Order object enters the Retrieving Books state, the object also enters the Accumulating from Inventory substate. If the system is able to retrieve all the books for the Order from inventory, the object leaves the Accumulating from Inventory substate *and* the Retrieving Books state and enters the Packaging state. On the other hand, if there are any books on back order, the Order enters the Waiting for Back Order substate, where it remains until the back-ordered books arrive.

At that point, the object enters the Accumulating from Back Order state, and at some point, the object leaves that substate and the enclosing state and enters the Packaging state. Regardless of what substate the object is in when it leaves the

Retrieving Books state, though, the last thing that happens is execution of the postToGL exit action.

Concurrent Substates

A *concurrent substate* is a substate in which an object can reside simultaneously with other substates at that same level within the given composite state. Given two or more composite substates at the same level, an object may be in one or more of them.

In this situation, two or more sets of substates can represent parallel flows of control. When the object enters a composite state with concurrent substates, the object also enters the initial states of each set of substates. Just like on an activity diagram, you can resynchronize these parallel flows. On a state diagram, however, you show this resynchronization by using a final state for each parallel set of concurrent substates.

Figure 7-18 shows how you use the UML to represent some concurrent substates that belong to the Shipping state, another one of the states in which an Order object can reside.

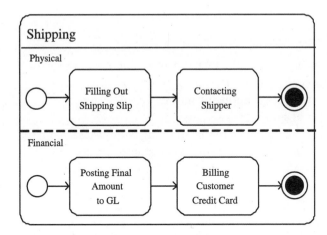

Figure 7-18. Concurrent substates

When an Order object enters the Shipping state, the object also enters the Filling Out Shipping Slip substate and the Posting Final Amount to GL substate at the same time. Work proceeds along both paths in parallel; there are no dependencies between the activities associated with the Physical path and those in the Financial path. Once the Order reaches the final states along both paths (represented by the "bull's-eyes"), the object leaves the Shipping state.

Note that Physical and Financial represent *regions* of the composite state Shipping, where each region contains its own concurrent substates and transitions.

Transitions in and out of composite states with concurrent substates work the same way as do transitions for states with sequential substates. You can also use a history state in conjunction with concurrent substates.

Here are some other relevant facts about sequential and concurrent substates:

- A substate within a composite state can have any or all of the details that can be associated with a regular state, such as entry actions, activities, and deferred events.

- A source state, which resides outside a given composite state, can have an associated transition whose target state is either the composite state as a whole or any one of the substates that compose that state. (If the target of the transition is the composite state itself, you start with the initial state symbol in tracing the flow.)

- Similarly, a transition can come out of a substate and then leave the enclosing composite state without having to go through the other substates.

Submachines

A *submachine* is a state machine that can be invoked as part of one or more other state machines. A *submachine state* is a state that references a submachine such that a copy of that submachine is implicitly part of the enclosing state machine where the reference occurs.

Within Figure 7-19, there is a reference to the Shipping composite state, which is partially defined in Figure 7-18. (A submachine state is semantically equivalent to the composite state defined by the referenced state machine.)

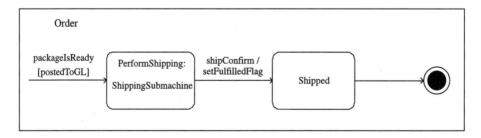

Figure 7-19. Submachine state

Note that an entry point or an exit point (see the section "Pseudostates," earlier in this chapter) can serve as a *connection point reference,* which represents a usage, as part of a given submachine state, of an entry point or exit point defined in the state machine that the submachine state references. The notation for a connection point reference is the same as that for a regular entry point or exit point.

Protocol State Machines

A *protocol state machine* specifies which operations of a given class can be called when instances of that class are in particular states and under which conditions. Thus, a protocol state machine specifies the allowable call sequences on the class's operations.

A protocol state machine is indicated by the {protocol} keyword next to the name on a state machine diagram (see the next section).

A *protocol transition* specifies that a given operation can be called for an instance of the given class in its initial state, under the initial condition specified as a precondition by a particular guard, and that at the end of the transition, the destination state will be reached under a specified postcondition, also specified as a guard.

The notation for a protocol transition is the same as that for a regular transition, except that a protocol transition does not specify an action.

The behavior of a protocol state machine is directed under an overall policy specified by a *protocol conformance.* This is the means by which the protocol state machine specifies a protocol that conforms to a more general state machine protocol, or that a specific behavioral state machine abides by the protocol of a more general protocol state machine. In particular, protocol conformance means that every rule and constraint specified for the general protocol state machine— including state invariants, preconditions, and postconditions for the operations it refers to—apply to the specific protocol or behavioral state machine. (An *invariant* specifies a condition that must always hold true under the relevant circumstances.)

State Machine Diagrams

A *state machine diagram* shows a state machine. The emphasis is the flow of control between states.

Figure 7-20 shows an excerpt from an example state machine diagram. (The use of an enclosing box and a name for the diagram are optional.)

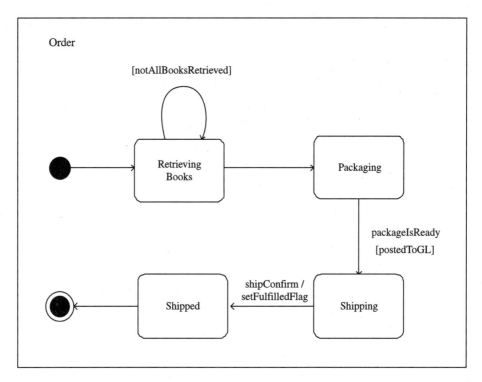

Figure 7-20. State machine diagram

Since state machine diagrams are generally done at the design level, it makes sense to put them into design-level packages, such as the one shown in Figure 7-21.

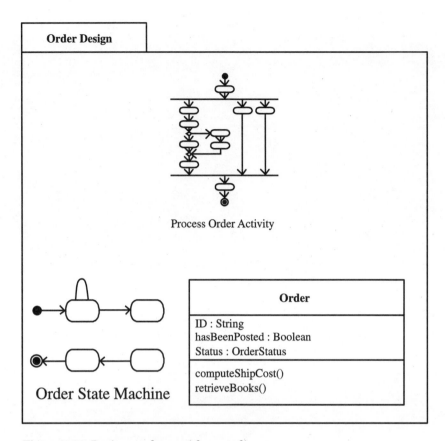

Order Design

Process Order Activity

Order

ID : String
hasBeenPosted : Boolean
Status : OrderStatus

computeShipCost()
retrieveBooks()

Order State Machine

Figure 7-21. Design package with state diagram

Looking Ahead

The next chapter shifts the focus back to a broader view of the dynamic behavior of a system, as it explores how the objects that comprise the system interact to perform the necessary behavior.

CHAPTER 8

Interactions

THIS CHAPTER DISCUSSES THE VARIOUS ASPECTS of interactions. The focus is on the messages that pass back and forth between objects during system execution.

Interactions, Lifelines, and Messages

An *interaction* is a behavior that focuses on the observable exchange of information between objects.

A *lifeline* represents the participation of a given object in a particular interaction. A lifeline appears on a sequence diagram (discussed in the section "Sequence Diagrams," later in this chapter) as a dashed line extending from the bottom of the object to which it belongs. Figure 8-1 shows two examples of lifelines.

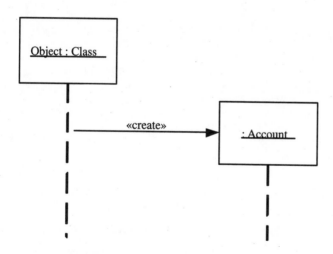

Figure 8-1. Lifelines

Objects communicate via *messages* between lifelines. The notation for a message is always an arrow, but the nature of the arrow and the arrowhead varies based on the type of message, as follows:

- A synchronous call or signal message appears as a solid line with a solid arrowhead.

- An asynchronous call or signal message appears as a solid line with a half-arrowhead.

- A reply message appears as a dashed line with a solid arrowhead.

- An object creation message appears as a dashed line with a feathered arrowhead.

- A "lost" message (one in which the sender is known but the receiver is not) has a small black circle next to the arrowhead.

- A "found" message (one in which the receiver is known but the sender is not) has a small black circle next to the start of the arrow.

Interaction Fragments

An *interaction fragment* is a distinct piece of an interaction. The following sub-sections describe the seven kinds of interaction fragments.

Combined Fragments

A *combined fragment* is a combination of one or more *interaction operands,* each of which contains one or more interaction fragments, and an *interaction operator,* which operates on those operands.

There are 12 types of interaction operators; they are described as follows:

- alt (The combined fragment represents a choice of behaviors: Each fragment has an associated guard, which means that at most one of the operands will execute.)

- assert (The combined fragment represents an assertion: The fragment must occur exactly as specified.)

- break (The combined fragment represents a breaking scenario: The operand is performed instead of the remainder of the enclosing interaction fragment.)

- consider (The combined fragment is designating which types of messages should be considered and which should be ignored.)

- critical (The combined fragment represents a critical region: The system ignores any interrupts until everything within the region has finished executing.)

- ignore (The combined fragment does not show at least one message type, which means that these message types can be considered insignificant and are ignored if they appear in a corresponding behavior execution.)

- loop (The combined fragment represents a loop: The loop operand is repeated the specified number of times.)

- neg (The combined fragment represents one or more messages defined to be invalid.)

- opt (The combined fragment represents a choice of behavior where either the sole operand happens or nothing happens, based on the evaluation of the associated guard.)

- par (The combined fragment represents a parallel merge between the behaviors of the operands: The different operands can be interleaved in any way.)

- seq (The combined fragment represents a "weak" sequencing between the behaviors of the operands, which means the following: [a] The ordering of messages within each of the operands is maintained in the result; [b] messages on different lifelines from different operands may come in any order; and [c] messages on the same lifeline from different operands are ordered such that a message within the first operand comes before that of the second operand.)

- strict (The combined fragment represents a strict sequencing between the behaviors of the operands.)

Figure 8-2 shows how a combined fragment, partially defined by the loop interaction operator, appears on a sequence diagram.

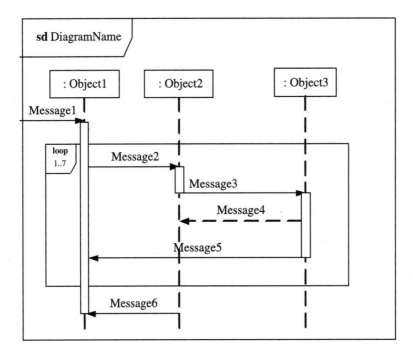

Figure 8-2. Combined fragment

Interaction operands are separated by dashed lines on a sequence diagram, as shown in Figure 8-3.

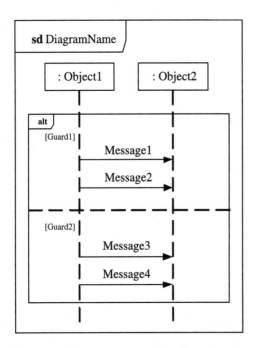

Figure 8-3. Interaction operands

Figure 8-3 shows two *interaction constraints;* these are Boolean expressions that guard operands within a combined fragment.

Continuations

A *continuation* defines a continuation of one branch of a combined fragment that is partially defined by the alt interaction operator.

Figure 8-4 shows how continuations appear on a sequence diagram.

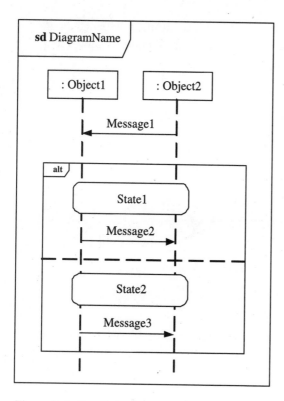

Figure 8-4. Continuations

If Object1 currently resides in State1, Object1 sends Message2 to Object2 while remaining in State1. If Object1 is in State2 instead, Object1 sends Message3 instead while remaining in State2.

Event Occurrences

An *event occurrence* represents a moment in time with which an action is associated. There are three kinds of event occurrences, described as follows:

- A *message end* represents what can occur at the end of a message in the context of a given interaction.

- A *gate* serves as a connection point for relating a message outside a given interaction fragment with a message inside the fragment.

- A *stop* defines the termination of the instance connected to a given lifeline. A stop appears as an X at the bottom of the lifeline, as shown in Figure 8-5.

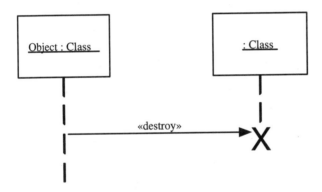

Figure 8-5. Stop

One can specify *general ordering* of two event occurrences: One must occur before the other within a given interaction.

Execution Occurrences

An *execution occurrence* represents the instantiation of a unit of a particular behavior on a lifeline, expressed in terms of a starting event occurrence (such as the receipt of a message) and an ending event occurrence (such as a reply to that message).

Interaction Occurrences

An *interaction occurrence* represents the occurrence of a piece of a particular interaction with specific values replacing the value placeholders defined for the interaction. Interaction occurrences are generally used to factor out common behavior that exists within a number of interactions.

Figure 8-6 shows how an interaction occurrence appears on a sequence diagram.

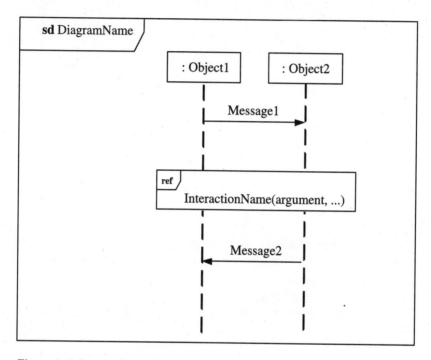

Figure 8-6. Interaction occurrence

Part Decompositions

A *part decomposition* describes the behavior of a part that belongs to the internal structure of some model element (see the section "Internal Class Structure" in Chapter 1).

Figure 8-7 shows how a part decomposition appears on a sequence diagram.

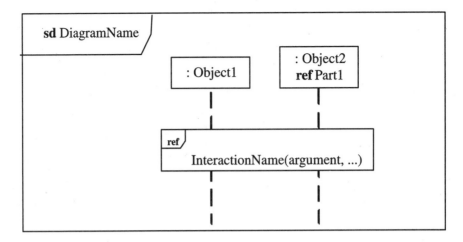

Figure 8-7. Part decomposition

The referenced interaction fragment is a description of some of the behavior associated with Part1, which belongs to the class to which Object2 belongs.

State Invariants

A *state invariant* serves as a runtime constraint on a given lifeline. The constraint is evaluated immediately before the next scheduled event occurrence (see the section "Event Occurrences," earlier in this chapter).

You model a state invariant using the same curly brackets as you would use for other constraints (see the section "More About Operations" in Chapter 1).

Interaction Diagrams

An *interaction diagram* shows aspects of an interaction. The following subsections describe the four kinds of UML interaction diagrams.

Sequence Diagrams

A *sequence diagram* focuses on the time-ordering of messages between objects. Figure 8-8 shows an example of a sequence diagram. (The use of an enclosing box and a name for the diagram is optional. The inclusion of the text for the use case with which this diagram corresponds is also optional.)

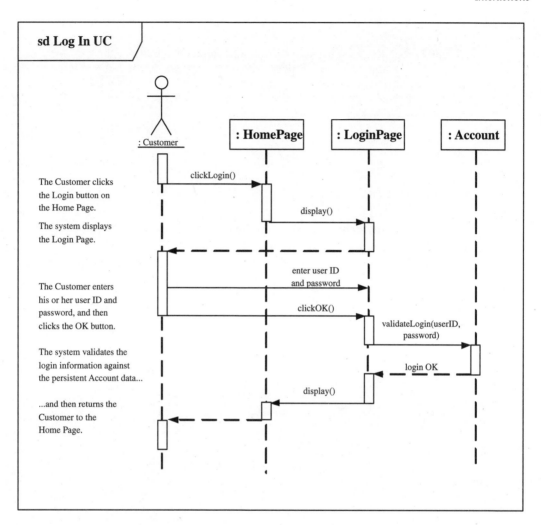

Figure 8-8. Sequence diagram

Sequence diagrams are excellent vehicles for working your way through use cases and allocating the required behavior to the participating objects. See *Use Case Driven Object Modeling with UML*[1] for more on this topic. Within the diagram, the use case text is aligned with the associated message(s) so the reader can see how the "how" (the design) matches with the "what" (the analysis). This improves the readability of the diagram and goes a long way toward ensuring that the requirements specified by the given use case are being met by the design.

---

[1] Doug Rosenberg with Kendall Scott, *Use Case Driven Object Modeling with UML* (Boston, MA: Addison-Wesley, 1999).

> **NOTE** Sequence diagrams and communication diagrams (see the next section) are semantically equivalent, which means you can convert one type of diagram to the other without losing any information. However, a sequence diagram has two key features that a communication diagram does not: lifelines and focuses of control.

Communication Diagrams

A *communication diagram* focuses on the interaction between lifelines, where the architecture of the internal structure and how this corresponds with the message passing is central. The messages are usually notated with *sequence numbers*, which indicate the relative execution order of the associated messages.

Figure 8-9 shows an excerpt from an example communication diagram.

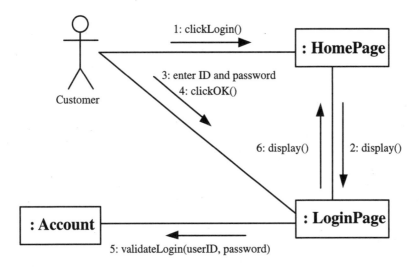

Figure 8-9. Communication diagram

As mentioned earlier in the chapter, the frame and the figure title are optional.

> **NOTE** Communication diagrams and sequence diagrams (see the section "Sequence Diagrams," earlier in this chapter) are semantically equivalent, which means that you can convert one type of diagram to the other without losing any information. A sequence diagram does not have sequence numbers, but it has a number of features that communication diagrams do not offer.

Since both sequence diagrams and communication diagrams are done at the design level, it makes sense to put them into design-level packages, such as the one shown in Figure 8-10.

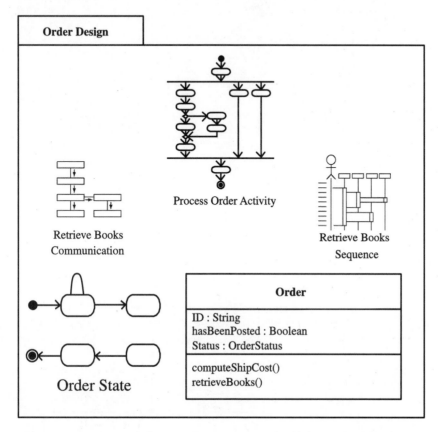

Figure 8-10. Design package with sequence and collaboration diagrams

Interaction Overview Diagrams

An *interaction overview diagram* focuses on the overview of the flow of control within a given interaction. This type of diagram resembles an activity diagram (see the section "Activity Diagrams" in Chapter 6) in that interactions and/or interaction occurrences serve as the activity nodes. All other symbols that appear on sequence diagrams and activity diagrams can appear on interaction overview diagrams.

Figure 8-11 shows an example of what might appear on an interaction overview diagram.

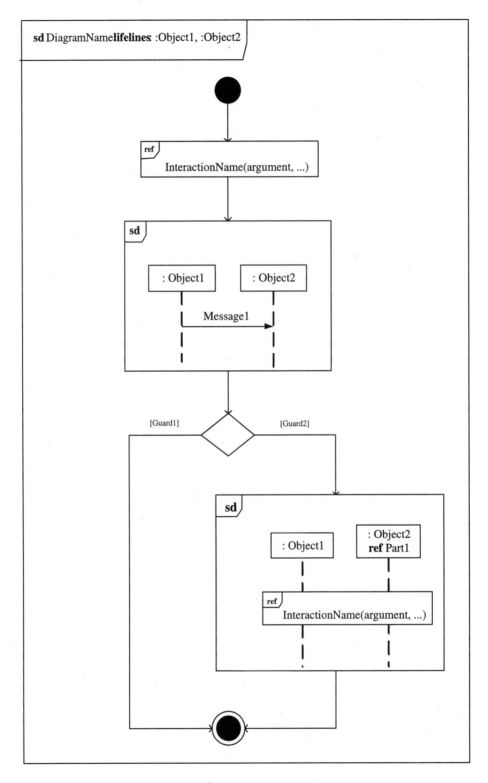

Figure 8-11. Interaction overview diagram

Timing Diagrams

A *timing diagram* describes the behavior of both individual objects and interactions of those objects, focusing attention on the times of occurrence of events that cause changes in state.

Figure 8-12 shows the elements of a typical timing diagram, as follows:

- Tick marks

- A *duration constraint* (This is a constraint on a *duration interval*, which represents the range between two given durations; see the section "Intermediate Read and Write Actions" in Chapter 6.)

- A *timing constraint* (This is a constraint on a *time interval*, which represents the range between two given time expressions; this interval is expressed in the form *first time..last time.*)

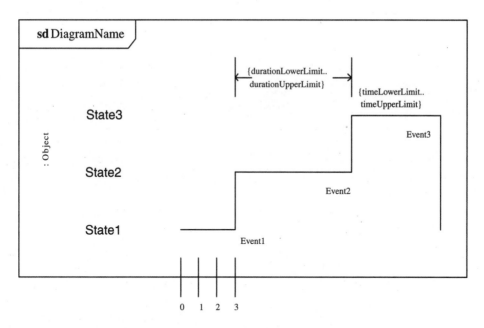

Figure 8-12. Timing diagram

Looking Ahead

The next chapter represents a move away from modeling the behavior of interacting objects and toward the modeling of larger groups of objects, in terms of how these groupings are defined and how the objects will be distributed across the system.

CHAPTER 9

Components, Deployment, and Higher-Level Modeling

THIS CHAPTER FOCUSES ON THE MODELING of autonomous units within a system or subsystem that the modeler can use to define software systems of arbitrary size and complexity. The chapter also describes the modeling of the deployment of those units. Finally, the chapter introduces three stereotypes that are useful in labeling packages that contain high-level models.

Components

A *component* is a named physical and replaceable part of a system that represents the physical packaging and implementation of otherwise logical elements (such as classes). This includes both logical components, such as business components and process components, and physical components, such as Enterprise Java Beans (EJBs), Common Object Request Broker Architecture (CORBA) components, and COM+ and .NET components.

Every component has a contractual obligation to conform to, and provide the realization of, one or more interfaces. As with classes, these are called *provided interfaces* (see the section "Interfaces, Ports, and Connectors" in Chapter 1). A component can also have required interfaces, as can classes.

Figure 9-1 shows an example of a component along with two each of provided interfaces and required interfaces.

Figure 9-2 shows an alternate notation that emphasizes the services that the component needs to call via its required interfaces.

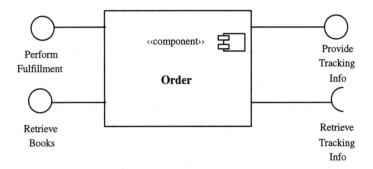

Figure 9-1. Component

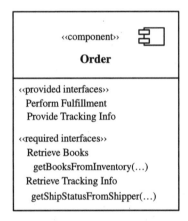

Figure 9-2. Component (alternate notation)

A component may also have ports (see the section "Interfaces, Ports, and Connectors" in Chapter 1).

A component is generally in a *realization* relationship with one or more classes that implement the interfaces that the component provides. This is the same kind of relationship that a class has with its interfaces; it's just at a lower level of abstraction. (Note that in this context, "implementation" implies a more refined or elaborate form of the client, *not* necessarily a physical implementation as, say, program code.) Figure 9-3 shows an example of a realization dependency.

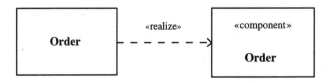

Figure 9-3. Realization dependency

Another way that component realization relationships can be depicted involves showing the realizing classes as properties of the component. The notation is comparable to that for the internal structure of classes (see the section "Internal Class Structure" in Chapter 1).

In the context of components, there are two types of connectors, described as follows:

- A *delegation connector* links the external contract of a component, as specified by its ports, to the internal realization of that behavior by the component's parts. You use delegation connectors to model the hierarchical decomposition of behavior, where services provided by a component may ultimately be realized by a part nested multiple levels deep.

- An *assembly connector* connects a required interface or a port on one component to a provided interface or port on another component. Assembly connectors are the primary mechanism for "wiring" components together on component diagrams (see the next section).

Component Diagrams

A *component diagram* focuses on a set of components and the structural relationships among them. The diagram may also show interfaces.

Figure 9-4 shows a set of Java Servlets that have been defined for a Web server using the «servlet» stereotype.

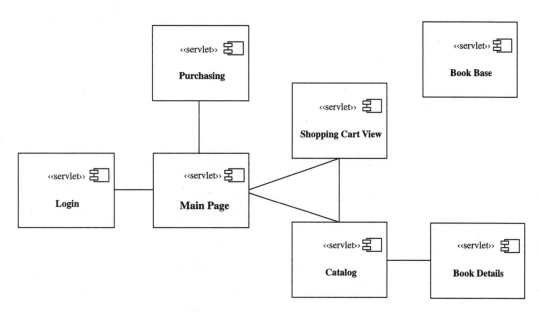

Figure 9-4. Component diagram for Web server

The elements of Figure 9-4 are as follows:

- **Book Details** retrieves the information, such as the thumbnail of the cover, the current price, and the various reviews that appear when the Customer wants to see the details about a particular Book.

- **Book Base** contains a cached list of all available Books; other servlets call this one when they need to retrieve information about particular Books.

- **Catalog** returns the results of Customer search and browse requests.

- **Login** handles Customer logins.

- **Main Page** is the first page a Customer sees when he or she gets to the bookstore's site.

- **Purchasing** handles the conversion of a Shopping Cart to an Order and also interacts with the external financial entities that approve or deny Customer credit cards.

- **Shopping Cart View** handles Customer modifications to the contents of Shopping Carts.

Figure 9-5 shows a set of components that have been defined on a separate application server.

The elements of this diagram are as follows:

- **Book** is an entity bean that contains a Book's ISBN, name, and author; a brief description of the Book; and the list price.

- **Cart Line Item** is a stateful session bean that contains a pointer to a particular Book in a Shopping Cart, the desired quantity of that Book, and the discount on the list price of that Book, as applicable.

- **Customer** is a stateful session bean that contains the key information necessary to log a Customer in and ship Orders to him or her.

- **Order** is an entity bean that contained information such as the total cost of an Order and the date it was placed; a Shopping Cart becomes an Order when the Customer gives final approval.

- **Order Line Item** is an entity bean that contains the same information as the associated Cart Line Item.

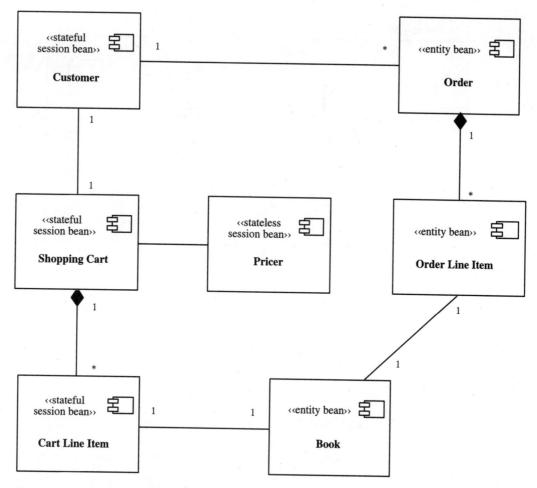

Figure 9-5. Component diagram for application server

- **Pricer** is a stateless session bean that calculates the cost for each Cart Line Item in a Customer's Shopping Cart, based on list prices, discounts, and quantities.

- **Shopping Cart** is a stateful session bean that contains pointers to the Books that the Customer wants to buy.

Note that some of the session beans described in the previous list are stateful, rather than stateless, to allow a Customer to retrieve the contents of his or her Shopping Cart even after an interruption in his or her session.

Component diagrams are generally put into their own packages, such as the one shown in Figure 9-6.

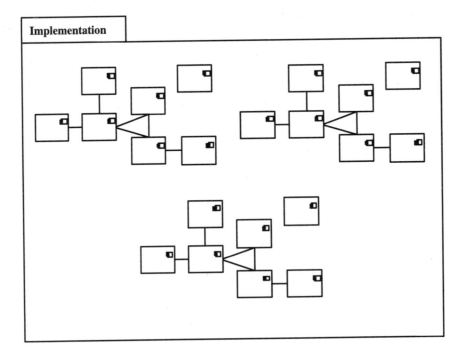

Figure 9-6. Implementation package

Component Stereotypes

The following built-in stereotypes may prove useful in helping you define components:

- The «entity» stereotype signifies persistent information related to a particular business concept.

- The «process» stereotype signifies that the component is transaction based.

- The «service» stereotype signifies that the component is stateless and that its only purpose is to compute some value.

- The «implement» stereotype signifies that the component implements a class identified by a specification (see the section "Other Stereotypes on Classes" in Chapter 1).

- The «buildComponent» stereotype, when assigned to a set of components, signifies that the components have been grouped for organizational or system-level development purposes.

Artifacts and Manifestations

An *artifact* represents a physical piece of information, such as a model, a file, or a table, that is used or produced by a software development process.

Figure 9-7 shows three example artifacts. One is represented using a user-defined icon, and the other two are shown as stereotyped classes.

Figure 9-7. Artifacts

An artifact can also contain other artifacts as part of a composition relationship (see the section "Aggregation" in Chapter 2).

A *manifestation* represents the concrete physical realization of one or more elements of a model by an artifact.

Figure 9-8 shows that the Order class is manifested by the Order.jar Java file from Figure 9-7.

Figure 9-8. Manifestation

Manifestation is a form of abstraction dependency; see the section "Abstraction Dependencies" in Chapter 2.

The following built-in stereotypes may prove useful in helping you define artifacts:

- The «document» stereotype signifies that the artifact contains useful information about the system being modeled. This information isn't part of any of the models themselves, and it doesn't take the form of source code (see the description of «source» later in this list) or an executable file (see the description of «executable» later in this list).

- The «executable» stereotype signifies that the artifact is a piece of executable software.

- The «file» stereotype signifies that the artifact is a physical file.

- The «library» stereotype signifies that the artifact contains a static or dynamic object library (for instance, a Windows Dynamic Link Library [DLL]).

- The «script» stereotype signifies that the artifact is a script file that can be interpreted by a system.

- The «source» stereotype signifies that the artifact contains source code.

Nodes

A *node* represents a computational resource that generally has memory and often has processing capability.

The notation for a node is a cube. The name of the node always appears on the cube; optionally, a list of the components that reside on that node also appears. Figure 9-9 shows two example nodes, connected with a communication path, which is comparable to an association between classes (see the section "Associations" in Chapter 2).

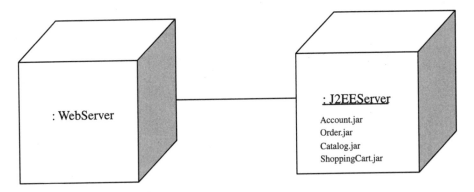

Figure 9-9. Nodes

The UML defines the following two specific kinds of nodes:

- A *device* is a physical computational resource with processing capability upon which artifacts may be deployed for execution. Figure 9-10 shows two example devices. (Listing the components that reside on the device is optional.)

Figure 9-10. Devices

A device may also contain other devices via a composition relationship (see the section "Aggregation" in Chapter 2).

- An *execution environment* offers an environment for the execution of specific types of components that are deployed on the environment, in the form of executable artifacts. Figure 9-11 shows an example of an execution environment.

Figure 9-11. Execution environment

Deployment

Nodes represent *deployment targets*—in other words, locations on which artifacts can be deployed. An artifact that exists on a particular node is called a *deployed artifact*; a *deployment* is the pairing of a deployed artifact with a deployment target.

The details of a deployment may appear in a *deployment specification*, which specifies a set of properties that determine the execution parameters of, say, a component deployed to a particular node. Figure 9-12 shows an example of a deployment specification.

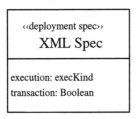

Figure 9-12. Deployment specification

Deployment Diagrams

A *deployment diagram* shows the configuration of a set of runtime processing nodes and, optionally, the artifacts that reside on them. Figure 9-13 shows an example that uses user-defined visual stereotypes.

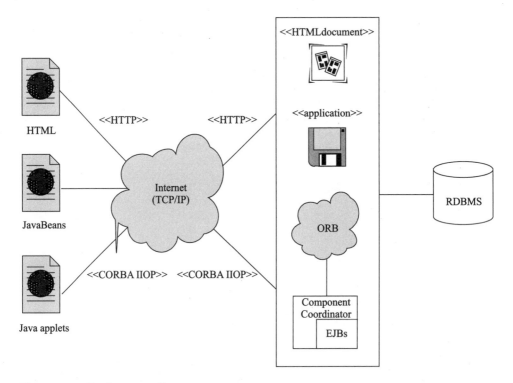

Figure 9-13. Deployment diagram

Deployment diagrams are generally put into their own packages, such as the one shown in Figure 9-14.

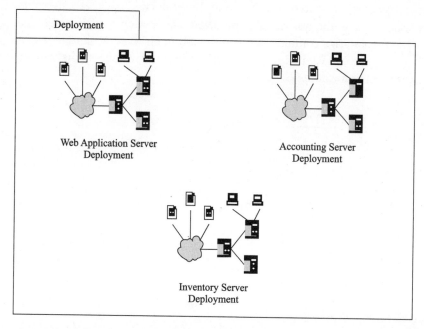

Figure 9-14. Deployment package

Frameworks, Subsystems, and Systems

You can use the «framework» stereotype to signify that the contents of a given package, taken together, represent an architectural pattern that provides an extensible template for applications within a domain.

Figure 9-15 shows an example of a framework.

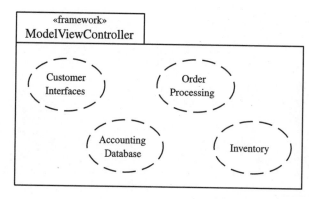

Figure 9-15. Framework

The Customer Interfaces collaboration represents the View portion of the pattern, Order Processing represents the Controller portion, and Accounting Database and Inventory represent the Model portion.

The «subsystem» stereotype signifies that the associated package represents an independent part of the system being modeled. The «systemModel» stereotype signifies that the package contains a collection of models that, taken together, model the entire system. Figure 9-16 shows three examples of subsystems "rolling up" to the system as a whole.

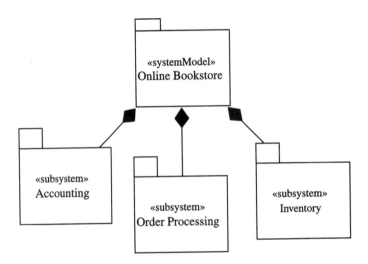

Figure 9-16. Subsystems

Looking Ahead

The next and final chapter takes a look at some features of UML 2.0 that don't quite fit in with the rest of the language: profiles, templates, and information flows.

CHAPTER 10

Profiles, Templates, and Information Flows

THIS CHAPTER DISCUSSES TOPICS THAT DON'T QUITE FIT into the preceding discussion, yet are important elements of the UML. The following topics are presented:

- Profiles, which are stereotyped packages that contain elements customized for a particular domain or purpose

- Templates, which provide ways to create families of model elements such as classes, packages, and collaborations

- Information flows, which provide ways to circulate information between objects at a fairly high level of abstraction

Profiles

A *profile* is a stereotyped package that contains model elements that have been customized for a particular platform (for example, J2EE or Microsoft .NET), domain (such as business process modeling), or purpose (for example, security thread modeling). The most common way to customize these elements involves the use of stereotypes.

Let's look at some of the contents of some sample profiles contained within the UML specification[1] and a separate profile also commissioned by the Object Management Group (OMG), which is the body responsible for ongoing work on the UML.

The example profile for Enterprise JavaBeans includes a number of stereotypes that have appeared in different forms in this book, including «EJBEntityBean»

---

[1] Object Management Group, *Unified Modeling Language: Superstructure, Version 2.0*, ptc/03-07-06.

(called «entity bean» in Figure 3-4) and «JAR» (called an «artifact» in Figure 9-8). Other stereotypes that might belong to an EJB profile include the following:

- «EJBMessageBean» (The component is invoked by the arrival of a message.)

- «EJBBusiness» (The method supports an element of business logic of the bean.)

- «EJBRoleName» (The actor is a security role used, for example, to define permissions for method invocations.)

The stereotypes presented for possible COM and .NET profiles include the following:

- «COMAtlClass» (The class is an ATL [Active Template Library] class that realizes a CoClass and provides its implementation.)

- «COMInterface» (The class is a component interface.)

- «COMDLL» (The artifact is a component library.)

- «NETAssembly» (The package is an assembly, which contains components and other necessary type definitions.)

See Rogerson[2] to learn more about COM and Chappell[3] to learn more about .NET.

The Software Process Engineering Metamodel (SPEM)[4] describes a foundation for defining a software development process. The specification, when expressed as a UML profile, defines a variety of stereotypes, including the following:

- «WorkProduct» (This is the rough equivalent of the UML's «artifact»; a work product is defined as anything produced, consumed, or modified by a process.)

---

[2] Dale Rogerson, *Inside COM: Microsoft's Component Object Model* (Seattle, WA: Microsoft Press, 1997).

[3] David Chappell, *Understanding .NET: A Tutorial and Analysis* (Boston, MA: Addison-Wesley, 2002).

[4] Object Management Group, *Software Process Engineering Metamodel Specification, Version 1.0,* formal/02-11-14.

- «WorkDefinition» (This describes an aspect of work performed within the process.)

- «Guidance» (This provides people with advice about how to use other elements of the model; subtypes of «Guidance» include «Guidelines» and «Examples».)

You can use the «apply» stereotype to signify that a given profile has been applied to a particular package. Figure 10-1 shows two example profile applications.

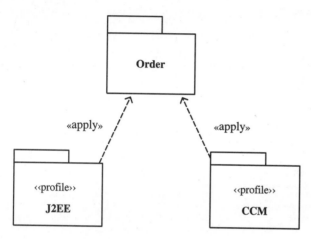

Figure 10-1. Profile applications

Note that CCM stands for CORBA Component Model.

On a related note, an *extension* is an association that indicates that the properties of a particular metaclass (see the section "Other Stereotypes on Classes" in Chapter 1) are extended through a particular stereotype.

Figure 10-2 shows how EJBHome (see the section "Design-Level Class Diagrams" in Chapter 3) serves to extend the UML metaclass Interface.

Figure 10-2. Extension

Templates

A *template* is a descriptor for a model element that has one or more formal parameters—basically, placeholders—that can be used to create a family of related model elements. You create a member of this family by *binding* actual parameters to the template's formal parameters. (The result of a binding is called a *bound element.*)

Within Figure 10-3, the Wish class is created via a binding to the Wish List template class.

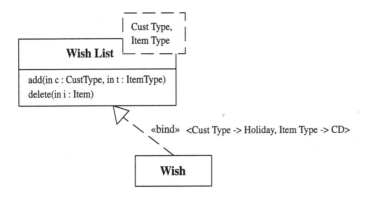

Figure 10-3. Binding

The dependency has the effect of creating a new Wish class that accepts Holiday customers (those who only make purchases at holiday time) who buy CDs (as opposed to books).

A package can also be bound to one or more template packages. Figure 10-4 shows an example of a bound package, which uses the elements that the package contains as its actual parameters.

The result of this binding is that the Shopping package contains Servlets named Login (the data entry page), Shopping Cart View (the page on which the Customer makes necessary edits), and Purchasing (a page hidden from Customers on which the Purchasing department does analysis related to Customer purchasing patterns).

Figure 1-22 (see Chapter 1) shows an example of a bound collaboration, which uses classes as its actual parameters. Figure 10-5 shows an alternate notation for this collaboration.

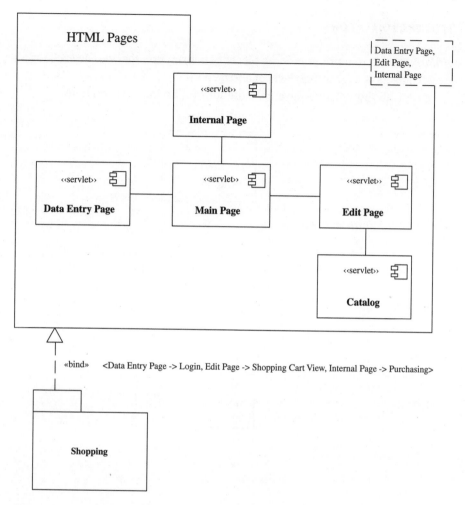

Figure 10-4. Bound package

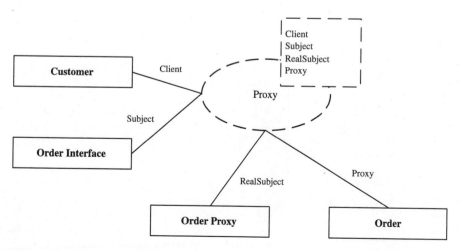

Figure 10-5. Bound collaboration

Information Flows

An *information item* represents some pieces of information that can be exchanged between objects at a fairly high level of abstraction.

Figure 10-6 shows two equivalent notations for an information item.

Figure 10-6. Information item

An *information flow* is a dependency within which one or more information items circulate from their sources to their targets. The flow doesn't specify the nature of the information or the mechanisms by which the information is conveyed.

Figure 10-7 shows an example of an information flow.

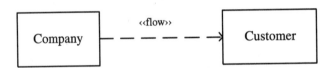

Figure 10-7. Information flow

Stereotypes

The following table lists all the built-in UML stereotypes referenced in this book.

STEREOTYPE	APPLIES TO	MEANING
«abstraction»	Dependency	The client is at one level of abstraction and the supplier is at a different level.
«access»	Dependency	The source package adds model elements that have private visibility from the target package.
«actor»	Class	The class is a role that a user can play with regard to a system or an entity, such as another system or a database, that resides outside the system.
«artifact»	Class	The class represents a physical piece of information, such as a model, a file, or a table, used or produced by a software development process.
«auxiliary»	Class	The class provides secondary logic or control flow.
«bind»	Dependency	The dependency binds a set of actual parameters to a template's formal parameters.
«buildComponent»	Component	The given set of components have been grouped for organizational or system-level development purposes.
«call»	Dependency	The source operation invokes the target operation.
«component»	Class	The class is a named physical and replaceable part of a system that represents the physical packaging and implementation of otherwise logical elements.
«create»	Dependency	The source class creates one or more instances of the target class.

STEREOTYPE	APPLIES TO	MEANING
«datastore»	Activity node	The node handles persistent information.
«dataType»	Class	The class is a set of values that have no identities and that can't be changed by operations.
«decisionInput»	Decision node	The associated node specifies the decision criterion for proceeding down each outgoing activity edge.
«deployment spec»	Class	The class specifies a set of properties that determine the execution parameters of, say, a component deployed to a particular node.
«derive»	Dependency	The client can be computed or inferred from the supplier.
«device»	Node	The node is a physical computational resource with processing capability upon which artifacts may be deployed for execution.
«document»	Artifact	The artifact contains useful information about the system being modeled that's not part of any of the models themselves.
«entity»	Component	The component holds persistent information related to a particular business concept.
«enumeration»	Class	The class is an ordered set of literals.
«executable»	Artifact	The artifact is executable software.
«execution environment»	Node	The node offers an environment for the execution of specific types of components that are deployed on it, in the form of executable artifacts.
«extend»	Dependency	The source use case implicitly includes the behavior of the target use case at one or more extension points.
«file»	Artifact	The artifact is a physical file of some kind.
«flow»	Dependency	One or more information items circulate from the source(s) to the target(s).
«focus»	Class	The class provides primary logic or control flow.

STEREOTYPE	APPLIES TO	MEANING
«framework»	Package	The contents of the package, taken together, represent an architectural pattern that provides an extensible template for applications within a domain.
«implement»	Component	The component implements a class identified by a specification (see «specification»).
«implementationClass»	Class	The class provides a static physical implementation of its objects.
«import»	Dependency	The source package adds model elements that have public visibility from the target package.
«include»	Dependency	The source use case explicitly includes the behavior of the target use case at a specified point within a course of action.
«information»	Class	The class represents some pieces of information that can be exchanged between objects at a fairly high level of abstraction.
«instantiate»	Dependency	One or more methods belonging to instances of the source class create instances of the target class.
«interface»	Class or Component	The stereotyped class or component is actually a collection of operations with no implementations.
«library»	Artifact	The artifact contains a static or dynamic object library (for instance, a Windows Dynamic Link Library [DLL])
«localPostcondition»	Action	The condition must hold true when execution of the action ends.
«localPrecondition»	Action	The condition must hold true when execution of the action begins.
«manifest»	Dependency	The target artifact represents the concrete physical realization of one or more source classes.
«metaclass»	Class	All instances of the class are themselves classes.

STEREOTYPE	APPLIES TO	MEANING
«modelLibrary»	Dependency	The client package is using the source package as a library of shared model elements.
«permit»	Dependency	The supplier grants the client permission to access some or all of its constituent elements.
«primitive»	Class	The class is a built-in data type.
«process»	Component	The component is transaction based.
«profile»	Package	The package contains model elements that have been customized for a particular platform, domain, or purpose.
«realize»	Dependency	The supplier serves as the implementation of the client.
«refine»	Dependency	The supplier is at a lower level of abstraction than the client.
«represents»	Dependency	A collaboration occurrence represents some behavior offered by a class.
«responsibility»	Dependency	The client has some kind of obligation to the supplier.
«script»	Artifact	The artifact is a script file that can be interpreted by a system.
«send»	Dependency	Instances of the source class send signals to instances of the target class.
«service»	Component	The component is stateless; its only purpose is to compute some value.
«signal»	Class	The class represents a request of some kind that an object belonging to that class dispatches asynchronously to one or more other objects.
«source»	Artifact	The artifact contains source code.
«specification»	Class	The class specifies the characteristics of a set of objects without defining the physical implementation of those objects.
«stereotype»	Class	The class is itself a stereotype that can be applied to other elements of a model.
«substitute»	Dependency	The client will comply with the contract specified by the supplier at program execution time.

STEREOTYPE	APPLIES TO	MEANING
«subsystem»	Package	The package represents an independent part of the system being modeled.
«systemModel»	Package	The package contains a collection of models that, taken together, model the entire system.
«trace»	Dependency	There is a conceptual connection among elements contained within different models.
«use»	Dependency	The client requires the presence of the supplier for its correct functioning or implementation.
«utility»	Class	The attributes and operations that belong to the class define data, or operate on data, for the class as a whole.

Glossary

abstract class	A *class* that can't have any *instances*.
abstraction dependency	A *dependency* within which the *client* is at one level of abstraction and the *supplier* is at a different level.
accept call action	An *action* that represents the receipt of a synchronous call request for an *operation* specified by a particular *call trigger*.
accept signal action	An *action* that waits for the occurrence of a *signal* of the type, or any subtype of that type, specified by a particular *signal trigger*.
accept time event action	An *action* that waits for an occurrence of a time *event* that meets the criteria specified by a particular *time trigger*.
access	A *dependency* within which the source *package* adds model elements that have private *visibility* from the target package.
action	An executable atomic assignment or computation that receives a set of input values and produces a change of *state* and/or the return of output values.
active class	A *class* that represents an independent flow of control, such as a process or a thread.
active object	An *instance* of an *active class*.
activity	An ongoing nonatomic (in other words, interruptible) execution of a series of *actions*.
activity diagram	A diagram that illustrates the flow(s) of control among *activities* and *actions* associated with a particular *object* or set of objects.
activity edge	A connection between *activity nodes*.
activity final node	A *final node* that terminates all flows within a given *activity*, and thus terminates the activity itself.
activity group	A grouping of *activity nodes* and *activity edges*.
activity node	A placeholder for one or more steps within an *activity*.

activity parameter node	A special type of *activity node* that appears at the beginning or end of a flow to accept inputs to an activity from another activity or to provide outputs from the activity to another activity.
activity partition	An *activity group* that identifies *actions* that have some characteristics in common.
actor	A role that a user can play with regard to a system or an entity, such as another system or a database, that resides outside the system.
add structural feature value action	An *action* that adds one or more values, specified on a particular *input pin*, to a specified structural feature.
add variable value action	An action that adds one or more values, specified on a particular *input pin*, to a given *variable*.
adornment	A piece of information that enhances an *association*.
aggregation	A special kind of *association* within which one or more "part" *classes* belong to a larger "whole" class.
alternate course of action	A path through a *use case* that represents an error condition or a path that the *actor* and the system take less frequently.
apply function action	An *action* that applies a specified *primitive function* to a set of values that the action retrieves from a specified *input pin*, and then places the return values on a specified *output pin*.
artifact	A physical piece of information, such as a model, a file, or a table, used or produced by a software development process.
assembly connector	A *connector* that connects a *required interface* or a *port* on one *component* to a *provided interface* or port on another component.
association	A simple structural connection between *classes*.
association class	An *association* that has interesting characteristics of its own outside of the *classes* it connects.
attribute	A named slot for a data value that belongs to a particular *class*.
basic course of action	The main start-to-finish path through a *use case* that the *actor* and the system follow under normal circumstances.

behavioral state machine	The specification of a sequence of *states* that an *object* goes through during its lifetime in response to *events* and also the responses that the objects makes to those events.
behavior port	A special kind of *port* that passes requests for specific behavior to the *instance* of the given *class* itself, rather than to any instances that the class may contain.
binary association	An *association* between two *classes*.
binding	A combination of actual parameters and a *template's* formal parameters.
bound element	The result of a *binding*.
broadcast signal action	An *action* that transmits an *instance* of a specified *signal* to a set of potential target *objects* in the system.
call behavior action	An *action* that invokes a specified behavior directly, either synchronously or asynchronously.
call dependency	A dependency within which the *source operation* invokes the *target* operation.
call operation action	An *action* that sends a *message* to a specified *object* to call a specified *method*, either synchronously or asynchronously.
call trigger	The reception of a request to call a specific *operation* belonging to a given *class* (which becomes a call on a *method* on an *object* that represents an *instance* of that class).
central buffer node	An *object node* that accepts *tokens* from "upstream" object nodes and passes them along to "downstream" object nodes.
change trigger	An *event* that occurs when a Boolean expression becomes True as a result of a change in value of one or more *attributes* or *associations*.
child	See *subclass*.
choice	A *pseudostate* that makes it possible to perform a branch within which the choice of which outgoing path to take can depend on the results of *actions* executed before the branch occurs as well as the *guards* connected with the branch.
class	A collection of *objects* that have the same characteristics.

class diagram	A diagram that focuses on a set of *classes* and the structural relationships among them; the diagram may also show *interfaces*.
clause	A combination of a test and a body section such that if execution of the test results in the Boolean value True, the body section is executed.
clear association action	An *action* that destroys all *links* that are *instances* of a particular *association* connected to an *object* specified on a particular *input pin*.
clear structural feature action	An *action* that deletes all values from a specified structural feature.
clear variable action	An *action* that deletes all values from a given *variable*.
client	The dependent element within a *dependency*.
collaboration	A description of a named structure of *classes*, *instances* of which each perform some specialized function (in other words, each serves a particular role).
collaboration occurrence	The application of the pattern described by a particular *collaboration* to a specific situation that involves specific *classes* or *instances* playing the roles of that collaboration.
combined fragment	A combination of one or more *interaction operands* and an *interaction operator*.
communication diagram	An *interaction diagram* that focuses on the *interaction* between *lifelines*, where the architecture of the internal structure and how this corresponds with the *message* passing are central.
complete action	An *action* that aggregates one or more *intermediate actions*.
component	A named physical and replaceable part of a system that represents the physical packaging and implementation of otherwise logical elements (such as *classes*).
component diagram	A diagram that focuses on a set of *components* and the structural relationships among them.
composite state	A *state* that has one or more nested *substates*.
composite structure diagram	A diagram that shows the internal structure of a *class* or *collaboration*.

composition	A "strong" form of *aggregation* within which if a particular *instance* of the whole is destroyed, so are the instances of the parts.
concurrency	A specification of how a *method* that implements a given *operation* responds in the context of multiple threads of activity.
concurrent substate	A *substate* in which an *object* can reside simultaneously with other substates at that same level within the given *composite state*.
conditional node	A *structured activity node* that represents an exclusive choice among some number of alternatives, each of which is expressed in the form of a *clause*.
connection point reference	A usage, as part of a given *submachine state*, of an *entry point* or *exit point* defined in the *state machine* that the submachine state references.
connector	Something that connects an *interface* to a *port*.
constraint	A specification of a condition that must hold true in a given context.
continuation	An *interaction fragment* that defines a continuation of one branch of a *combined fragment* partially defined by the alt *interaction operator*.
control flow	An *activity edge* that only passes control *tokens*.
control node	An *activity node* that coordinates flows among other activity nodes.
create dependency	A *dependency* within which the *source class* creates one or more *instances* of the *target* class.
create link action	An *action* that creates a *link* using the *association* ends specified by two or more *link end creation data* entities.
create link object action	An *action* that creates a *link object*, using the association ends, and perhaps the *qualifier* values, specified by two or more specified *link end creation data* entities, and then places the object on the specified *output pin*.
create object action	An *action* that creates an *object* belonging to a specified *class*, and then places that object on a particular *output pin*.
data store node	A special type of *central buffer node* that handles persistent information.

decision node	A *control node* that offers a choice among two or more outgoing *activity edges*, each of which has a *guard*.
deep history	A *pseudostate* that "remembers" the innermost nested *state* at any depth within a *composite state*.
deferred event	An *event* that's of interest to a given *object*, but which the object defers handling until the object reaches a different *state*.
delegation connector	A *connector* that links the external contract of a *component*, as specified by its *ports*, to the internal realization of that behavior by the component's *parts*.
dependency	A "using" relationship within which a change in one thing (such as a *class*) may affect another thing (for instance, another class).
deployed artifact	An *artifact* that exists on a particular *node*.
deployment	The pairing of a *deployed artifact* with a *deployment target*.
deployment specification	The specification of a set of properties that determine the execution parameters of, say, a *component* deployed to a particular *node*.
deployment target	A location on which *artifacts* can be deployed.
derivation dependency	A *dependency* within which the *client* can be computed or inferred from the *supplier*.
destroy link action	An *action* that creates a *link* or *link object* using the *association* ends specified by two or more *link end data* entities.
destroy object action	An *action* that destroys an *object* specified on a particular *input pin*.
device	A node that represents a physical computational resource with processing capability upon which *artifacts* may be deployed for execution.
duration	The length of time between the occurrence of two particular *events*.
duration constraint	A constraint on a *duration*.
duration interval	The range between two given *durations*.
duration observation action	An *action* that measures a *duration* during system execution.

encapsulation	The principle of data hiding: An *object* hides its data from the rest of the world and only lets outsiders manipulate that data by way of calls to the object's *methods*.
entry action	An *action* that a given *object* always performs immediately upon entering a given *state*.
entry point	A *pseudostate* that represents a point of entry into a *state machine*.
event	Something of significance to one or more *objects* that may cause the execution of some behavior associated with the object(s).
event occurrence	A moment in time with which a particular *action* is associated.
exception	A special kind of *signal* that an *object* can throw or receive in response to a failure during system execution.
exception handler	An entity that specifies an *executable node* to execute in case a specified *exception* occurs during the execution of another executable node.
exceptional flow of events	See *alternate course of action*.
executable node	An *activity node* that may be executed.
execution environment	A *node* that offers an environment for the execution of specific types of *components* that are deployed on it, in the form of executable *artifacts*.
execution occurrence	The instantiation of a unit of a particular behavior on a *lifeline*, expressed in terms of a starting *event occurrence* (such as the receipt of a *message*) and an ending *event occurrence* (such as a reply to that message).
exit action	An *action* that a given *object* always performs immediately before leaving a given *state*, in response to a regular *transition* or a *self-transition*.
exit point	A *pseudostate* that represents a point of exit from a *state machine*.
expansion node	An *object node* that indicates a flow across the boundary of an *expansion region*.
expansion region	A *structured activity node* that executes once for each element within a given collection of values in a particular *expansion node*.

extend	A *dependency* within which a base *use case* implicitly includes the behavior of another use case at one or more *extension points*.
extension	An *association* that indicates that the properties of a particular metaclass are extended through a particular *stereotype*.
extension point	A point within a base *use case* at which the use case implicitly includes the behavior of another use case within an *extend dependency*.
final node	A *control node* at which one or more flows within a given *activity* stop.
final state	A *pseudostate* that indicates that the execution of part or all of an enclosing *composite state*, or of an entire *state machine*, is complete.
flow final node	A *final node* that terminates a particular flow.
fork	A *pseudostate* that splits a *transition* into two or more transitions.
fork node	A *control node* that splits a flow into multiple concurrent flows.
gate	A connection point for relating a *message* outside a given *interaction fragment* with a message inside the fragment.
generalization	A relationship between a general *class* and a more specific version of that *class*, where the more specific class is a "kind of" the more general class.
generalization set	A specification of partitions for the *subclasses* of a particular *superclass*.
general ordering	The specification that one *event occurrence* must occur before another within a given *interaction*.
grammatical inspection	See *noun/verb analysis*.
guard	A Boolean expression that must resolve to True before the associated path along an *activity edge* can be taken.
import	A *dependency* within which the source *package* adds model elements that have *public visibility* from the target package.

include	A *dependency* within which one *use case* explicitly includes the behavior of another use case at a specified point within a course of action.
information flow	A *dependency* within which one or more *information items* circulate from their *sources* to their *targets*.
information item	A *stereotyped class* that specifies some pieces of information that can be exchanged between *objects* at a fairly high level of abstraction.
initial node	The *activity node* at which the flow of control starts when a given *activity* is invoked.
initial state	A *pseudostate* that indicates the default starting place for a *transition* whose *target* is the boundary of a *state*.
input pin	A *pin* that receives input values for an *action*.
instance	An *object* that belongs to a particular *class*, a *link* that belongs to a particular *association*, or a *link object* that belongs to a particular *association class*.
instantiation dependency	A *dependency* within which one or more *methods* belonging to *instances* of the *source class* create instances of the *target* class.
interaction	A behavior that focuses on the observable exchange of information between *objects*.
interaction constraint	A Boolean expression that *guards* an *interaction operand* within a *combined fragment*.
interaction diagram	A diagram that shows aspects of an *interaction*.
interaction fragment	A distinct piece of an *interaction*.
interaction occurrence	The occurrence of a piece of a particular *interaction* with specific values replacing the value placeholders defined for the interaction.
interaction operand	An operand that contains one or more *interaction fragments*.
interaction operator	An operator that operates on one or more *interaction operands*.
interaction overview diagram	An *interaction diagram* that focuses on the overview of the flow of control within a given *interaction*.
interface	A collection of *operations* that represent services offered by a *class* or a *component*.

intermediate action	An action primitive that carries out a computation or accesses *object* memory.
internal transition	A *transition* that leaves a given *object* in its current *state*.
interruptible activity region	An *activity group* that supports interrupts by terminating any *tokens* and behaviors connected with the *activity nodes* within the region when an interrupt arrives.
invariant	A *constraint* that specifies a condition that must always hold true under the relevant circumstances.
join	A *pseudostate* that merges two or more *transitions*.
join node	A *control node* that synchronizes multiple control flows.
junction	A *pseudostate* that makes it possible to build a single overall *transition* from a series of transition fragments.
lifeline	An entity that represents the participation of a given *object* in a particular *interaction*.
link	An *instance* of an *association* (in other words, a structural connection between *objects*).
link end creation data	An entity that specifies an *association* end that is subsequently used by a *create link action*.
link end data	An entity that specifies a *link* or *link object* that is subsequently used by a *destroy link action*.
link object	An instance of an association class.
local postcondition	A condition that must hold true when execution of an associated *action* ends.
local precondition	A condition that must hold true when execution of an associated *action* begins.
loop node	A *structured activity node* that represents a loop with setup, test, and body sections, within which the setup section is executed once on entry to the loop and the test and body sections are executed repeatedly until the test produces `False`.
main flow of events	See *basic course of action*.
manifestation	A *dependency* within which a *target artifact* represents the concrete physical realization of one or more *source classes*.

merge node	A *control node* that brings together multiple alternate control flows.
message	A communication between two *objects*, or within an object, that is designed to result in some activity.
message end	Something that can occur at the end of a *message* in the context of a given *interaction*.
method	An implementation of an *operation*.
multiplicity	An indication of how many of one thing can exist relative to another thing.
n-ary association	An *association* among three or more *classes*.
node	A computational resource that generally has memory and often has processing capability.
note	A device for recording comments about a model without affecting the content of the model.
noun/verb analysis	A technique for discovering *classes* that involves poring through high-level requirements documents, marketing materials, and other materials that provide insight into the problem domain.
object	A thing or concept that belongs to a particular *class*.
object diagram	A diagram that shows a set of *objects*, and the relationships among them, at a particular point in time during the execution of the system.
object flow	An *activity edge* that can have *objects* or data passing along it in addition to control *tokens*.
object node	An *activity node* that provides and accepts *objects* and data as they flow into and out of invoked behaviors in the context of the execution of an *activity*.
operation	A service that an *object* can request to affect behavior.
output pin	A *pin* that receives output values for an *action*.
package	A grouping of pieces of a model.
package diagram	A diagram that shows the contents of a *package*, which can include nested packages and, optionally, the relationships among those contents.
package visibility	A specification that *objects* belonging to any *class* in the same *package* as the given class can see and use that class.

parent	See *superclass*.
part	An *object* that a *class* contains by *composition*.
part decomposition	The description of the behavior of a *part* that belongs to the internal structure of some model element.
permission dependency	A *dependency* within which the *supplier* grants the *client* permission to access some or all of its constituent elements.
pin	A modeling element connected with an input to or output from an *action*.
port	A group of *provided interfaces* and/or *required interfaces* that specifies a distinct interaction point between a *class* or *component* and its environment.
postcondition	The specification of a condition that must hold true before a *method* starts executing.
powertype	A *class* within a *generalization set* whose *instances* are also *subclasses* of another class.
precondition	The specification of a condition that must hold true before a *method* starts executing.
primitive function	A predefined mathematical function, specified in an external language, that depends only on input values, as opposed to values from memory or *objects*.
private visibility	A specification that only *objects* belonging to a given *class* itself can use a particular *attribute* or *operation*.
profile	A *stereotyped package* that contains model elements that have been customized for a particular platform, domain, or purpose.
property	An *object* that a *class* references or owns.
protected visibility	A specification that only *objects* that belong to *subclasses* of a given *class* (at any level below that class) can use a particular *attribute* or *operation*.
protocol conformance	The means by which a *protocol state machine* specifies a protocol that conforms to a more general state machine protocol, or that a specific *behavioral state machine* abides by the protocol of a more general protocol state machine.

protocol state machine	A specification of which *operations* of a given *class* can be called when *instances* of that class are in particular *states* and under which conditions.
protocol transition	An entity that specifies that a given *operation* can be called for an *instance* of the given *class* in its initial *state*, under the initial condition specified as a *precondition* by a particular *guard*, and that at the end of the *transition*, the *target state* can be reached under a specified *postcondition*, also specified as a guard.
provided interface	An interface that a *class* or a *component* provides to potential clients for the *operations* that the class or component offers.
pseudostate	An entity that takes the basic form of a *state*, but that doesn't behave like a full state.
public visibility	A specification that *objects* belonging to any *class* can use a given *attribute* or *operation*.
qualifier	An *attribute* that defines a partition of a set of *instances* with respect to the *object* at the other end of a *link*.
raise exception action	An *action* that turns the value on the specified *input pin* into an *exception*.
read extent action	An *action* that retrieves all runtime *instances* of a specified *class* that are currently in existence, and then places this "extent" on a particular *output pin*.
read is classified object action	An *action* that determines whether an *object*, specified on a particular *input pin*, belongs to a particular *class*, and then places True if it is, or False if it isn't, on a particular *output pin*.
read link action	An *action* that navigates across a *link*, specified by two *link end data* entities, to retrieve the *object*(s) at one end, and then places the object(s) on a particular *output pin*.
read link object end action	An *action* that reads the *link object*, specified on a particular *input pin*, at a specified end, and then places the *object* on the specified *output pin*.
read link object end qualifier action	An *action* that reads the value of a specified *qualifier*, connected with a *link object* specified on a particular *input pin*, and then places the qualifier value on the specified *output pin*.

read self action	An *action* that retrieves the *object* to which the enclosing *activity* belongs and then places the object on a particular *output pin*.
read structural feature action	An *action* that retrieves the values of a specified structural feature and then puts these values on a particular *output pin*.
read variable action	An *action* that reads the values of a given *variable* and then puts these values on a specified *output pin*.
realization	What a *class* or *component* does for one or more *interfaces*.
realization dependency	A *dependency* within which the *supplier* serves as the implementation of the *client*.
reception	A declaration that a particular *class* or *interface* is prepared to react to the receipt of a given *signal*.
reclassify object action	An *action* that changes the *class*(es), from a specified "old" set to a specified "new" set, to which an *object*, specified on a particular *input pin*, belongs.
refinement	A *dependency* within which the *supplier* is at a lower level of abstraction than the *client*.
regions	A part of a *composite state* that contains its own *concurrent substates* and *transitions*.
remove structural feature value action	An *action* that deletes a value, specified on a particular *input pin*, from a specified structural feature.
remove variable value action	An *action* that deletes a value, specified on a particular *input pin*, from a given *variable*.
reply action	An *action* that accepts a set of return values and a token that contains return information, produced by a previous *accept call action*, from the specified *input pin*, and then places the values and the token on the specified *output pin*.
required interface	An interface that a *class* or *component* needs to fulfill its duties.
responsibility	An obligation that one *class* has with regard to other classes.
responsibility dependency	A *dependency* within which the *client* has some kind of obligation to the *supplier*.

role	A face that a *class* presents to other classes in the context of an *association*.
self-transition	A *transition* whose *source state* and *target state* are the same.
send dependency	A *dependency* within which *instances* of the *source class* send *signals* to instances of the *target* class.
send object action	An *action* that transmits a specified *object* to a specified target object as a *signal*.
send signal action	An *action* that creates an *instance* of a specified *signal* and transmits this instance to a specified target *object*.
sequence diagram	An *interaction diagram* that focuses on the time ordering of *messages* between *objects*.
sequence number	A number that indicates the relative execution order of the associated *message* on a *communication diagram*.
sequential substate	A *substate* in which an *object* can reside to the exclusion of all other substates at that same level within the given *composite state*.
shallow history	A *pseudostate* that "remembers" only the outermost nested *state* that a given *object* was in before it left the enclosing *composite state*.
signal	A request of some kind that an *object* dispatches asynchronously to one or more other objects.
signal trigger	The reception of a particular *signal*.
simple state	A *state* that has no nested *substates*.
source	See *client*.
source state	The "from" state within a *transition*.
start owned behavior action	An *action* that starts the behavior owned by the *object* specified on a particular *input pin*.
state	A condition in which an *object* can be at some point during its lifetime, for some finite amount of time.
state invariant	A runtime *constraint* on a given *lifeline*.
state machine diagram	A diagram that shows a *state machine*, with the emphasis on the flow of control between *states*.

stereotype	A mechanism for building a modeling construct that isn't identified in the core UML but that's similar to things that are part of the core.
stop	The termination of the *instance* connected to a given *lifeline*.
structured activity node	An *executable node* that represents a structured portion of a given *activity* that isn't shared with any other structured node, except for nodes that are nested.
subclass	The more specific *class* within a *generalization*.
submachine	A *state machine* that can be invoked as part of one or more other state machines.
submachine state	A *state* that references a *submachine* such that a copy of that submachine is implicitly part of the enclosing *state machine* where the reference occurs.
substates	A *state* nested within a *composite state*.
substitution	A *dependency* within which the *client* must comply with the contract specified by the *supplier* at program execution time.
superclass	The more general *class* within a *generalization*.
supplier	The independent element within a *dependency*.
swimlane	A pair of parallel vertical or horizontal lines on an *activity diagram* that represent an *activity partition*.
target	See *supplier*.
target state	The "to" state within a *transition*.
template	A descriptor for a model element that has one or more formal parameters that can be used to create a family of related model elements.
terminate	A *pseudostate* that represents the termination of the execution of a *state machine*.
test identity action	An *action* that determines whether two values, specified on separate *input pins*, refer to the same specified *object*, and then places True if they do, or False if they don't, on a particular *output pin*.
time interval	The range between two given time expressions.
time observation action	An *action* that measures the current time, according to the system clock, during system execution.

time trigger	An *event* that occurs after a specified period of time.
timing constraint	A constraint on a *time interval*.
timing diagram	An *interaction diagram* that describes the behavior of both individual *objects* and *interactions* of those objects, focusing attention on the times of occurrence of *events* that cause changes in *state*.
token	An entity that controls the flow of data and/or control within an *activity*.
trace	A *dependency* within which there is a conceptual connection among elements contained within different models.
transition	A change of an *object* from one *state* (the *source state*) to another *state* (the *target state*).
trigger	An occurrence of an *event*.
triggerless transition	A transition that fires unconditionally when the given *object* is ready to move from one *state* to another.
usage dependency	A dependency within which the *client* requires the presence of the *supplier* for its correct functioning or implementation.
use case	A sequence of actions performed by an *actor* and the system that yields an observable result, or set of results, of value for one or more actors.
use case instance	A unique execution of a *use case*.
variable	An element for passing data between *actions* indirectly.
visibility	A specification of whether something outside of a particular *object* or *package* can "see" something inside that object or package.

Bibliography

Scott Ambler, *Agile Database Techniques: Effective Strategies for the Agile Software Developer* (New York, NY: John Wiley & Sons, 2003).

David Bellin and Susan Suchman Simone, *The CRC Card Book* (Boston, MA: Addison-Wesley, 1997).

David Chappell, *Understanding .NET: A Tutorial and Analysis* (Boston, MA: Addison-Wesley, 2002).

Erich Gamma, Richard Helm, Ralph Johnson, and John Vlissides, *Design Patterns: Elements of Reusable Object-Oriented Software* (Boston, MA: Addison-Wesley, 1995).

Yun-Tung Lau, *The Art of Objects: Object-Oriented Design and Architecture* (Boston, MA: Addison-Wesley, 2001).

Dale Rogerson, *Inside COM: Microsoft's Component Object Model* (Seattle, WA: Microsoft Press, 1997).

Ed Roman, *Mastering Enterprise JavaBeans (Second Edition)* (New York, NY: John Wiley & Sons, 2001).

Doug Rosenberg with Kendall Scott, *Use Case Driven Object Modeling with UML* (Boston, MA: Addison-Wesley, 1999).

Object Management Group, *Software Process Engineering Metamodel Specification, Version 1.0,* formal/02-11-14.

Object Management Group, *Unified Modeling Language: Superstructure, Version 2.0,* ptc/03-07-06.

Rebecca Wirfs-Brock, Brian Wilkerson, and Lauren Wiener, *Designing Object-Oriented Software* (Englewood Cliffs, NJ: Prentice Hall, 1990).

Index

forums.apress.com

JOIN THE APRESS FORUMS AND BE PART OF OUR COMMUNITY. You'll find discussions that cover topics of interest to IT professionals, programmers, and enthusiasts just like you. If you post a query to one of our forums, you can expect that some of the best minds in the business—especially Apress authors, who all write with *The Expert's Voice™*—will chime in to help you. Why not aim to become one of our most valuable participants (MVPs) and win cool stuff? Here's a sampling of what you'll find:

DATABASES
Data drives everything.

Share information, exchange ideas, and discuss any database programming or administration issues.

PROGRAMMING/BUSINESS
Unfortunately, it is.

Talk about the Apress line of books that cover software methodology, best practices, and how programmers interact with the "suits."

INTERNET TECHNOLOGIES AND NETWORKING
Try living without plumbing (and eventually IPv6).

Talk about networking topics including protocols, design, administration, wireless, wired, storage, backup, certifications, trends, and new technologies.

WEB DEVELOPMENT/DESIGN
Ugly doesn't cut it anymore, and CGI is absurd.

Help is in sight for your site. Find design solutions for your projects and get ideas for building an interactive Web site.

JAVA
We've come a long way from the old Oak tree.

Hang out and discuss Java in whatever flavor you choose: J2SE, J2EE, J2ME, Jakarta, and so on.

SECURITY
Lots of bad guys out there—the good guys need help.

Discuss computer and network security issues here. Just don't let anyone else know the answers!

MAC OS X
All about the Zen of OS X.

OS X is both the present and the future for Mac apps. Make suggestions, offer up ideas, or boast about your new hardware.

TECHNOLOGY IN ACTION
Cool things. Fun things.

It's after hours. It's time to play. Whether you're into LEGO® MINDSTORMS™ or turning an old PC into a DVR, this is where technology turns into fun.

OPEN SOURCE
Source code is good; understanding (open) source is better.

Discuss open source technologies and related topics such as PHP, MySQL, Linux, Perl, Apache, Python, and more.

WINDOWS
No defenestration here.

Ask questions about all aspects of Windows programming, get help on Microsoft technologies covered in Apress books, or provide feedback on any Apress Windows book.

HOW TO PARTICIPATE:
Go to the Apress Forums site at **http://forums.apress.com/**.
Click the New User link.